W9-BSL-420

Only Love Can Save Us

Pope Francis

# Only Love Can Save Us

### Letters, Homilies, and Talks of Cardinal Jorge Bergoglio

Translated
by Gerard Seromik

Our Sunday Visitor Publishing Division
Our Sunday Visitor, Inc.
Huntington, Indiana 46750

Copyright © 2013 by Our Sunday Visitor Publishing Division, Our Sunday Visitor, Inc. Published 2013

18 17 16 15 14 13     1 2 3 4 5 6 7 8 9

ISBN: 978-1-61278-741-1 (Inventory No. T1552)
eISBN: 978-1-61278-343-7
LCCN: 2013948682

Cover design: Amanda Falk
Cover art: Newscom
Interior design: M. Urgo

PRINTED IN THE UNITED STATES OF AMERICA

# Contents

*Editor's note: Cardinal Jorge Mario Bergoglio, S.J., presented the material contained in this collection of writings before he was elected pontiff in March 2013.*

# INTRODUCTION

With the arrival of a new pope to the throne of Peter, Pope Francis, the Church is experiencing a special time of grace.

The pope is important to the faithful; he matters a lot. He is important as a person, and his mission is important to the faithful, because they care about the Church, they understand that he is the guarantee of the faith, the bedrock upon which the Church rests and finds its support. Moreover, they sense and they know that, by remaining united with Peter, in a communion of faith with him and under him, their proclamation of Jesus Christ is genuine and possible, and the poor — there is no greater poverty than not to believe — will believe or will remain faithful to the faith they have received, and the poor, the sinners, and the humble of heart will continue to receive the good news that God loves them and will not withdraw his unlimited mercy from them.

We recognize the successor of Peter in Pope Francis, as well as the visible sign of the unity of the Church, which is spread throughout the world. He is the cornerstone for the mission, the message, and the tradition of the Church.

He presides in charity over the whole Church, and is the guarantee of the Catholic and Apostolic Church to the truth — fully and irrevocably revealed in Jesus Christ, the one foundation and cornerstone of the Church — so that in all churches the true voice of its sole Shepherd, Jesus Christ, will be heard.

The name that he chose, Francis, best describes the new pope: a man of God, a man of faith, who passionately loves the Church and desires a Church that is renewed and holy; a humble and simple person; a man of the Gospel; a man of the Beatitudes, which proclaim blessed the poor and the suffering. He is a person who lives out poverty, who loves the poor, and who is with them and for them. Truly, he is a man who is free.

His choice of the name Francis, in memory of the Poverello of Assisi, is both a sign and a vocation for the Church and for the world. It is at once a plan for his life and a plan of action. We need a Francis of Assisi to inject into the world the freshness that comes from an evangelical lifestyle and from following Jesus in the only way possible: through the Cross and through the Beatitudes.

The Holy Father is also known for his great compassion and for his deep sense of prayer. He is very concerned about connecting with the heart of common and ordinary people. He is kind but firm when circumstances require it, yet always ready to accompany the sick, the poor, and those who suffer in any way.

I think the Holy Father has a personality and a heartfelt burden that leads him to deep reflection, as well as a simple and spontaneous way of saying things. Of course, simplicity and humility are not incompatible with firmness. Moreover, if, as St. Teresa of Avila used to say, "Humility is walking in truth," the pope's humility is made transparent in truth, in the proclamation and defense of the truth, accompanied by charity. As the Jesuit provincial of the Society of Jesus in Argentina, as the auxiliary bishop and archbishop of Buenos Aires, he has been a man of truth, and acted decisively in accordance with the truth by making important decisions and not acting halfheartedly. His love and devotion to the poorest of the poor is inconceivable without the firmness of truth that makes us free.

He is a man of God, simple, humble, poor, and a friend of the poor; a follower of Jesus, who follows Our Lord in the only way possible — with the Cross — by shedding all, imitating him, and reflecting the face that Jesus himself has given us in the Beatitudes. He is a faithful servant, a servant who does not seek his glory, but God's glory, and the well-being of those whom God, in his infinite mercy, loves with a special love and forgives unceasingly.

He is a man of prayer who has told us that authenticity comes from the Cross, from the love, mercy, and simplicity that flow from the Cross, in order to respond to what is always at the center of the Church's life: a material and spiritual poverty that is foreign to any purely simplistic interpretation.

Pope Francis, through many signs, has manifested a desire to bring others to this closeness and to this depth, which he himself has received in his life of prayer. These characteristics of his personality have made a deep impact upon us in these first few days of his pontificate.

The reaction of the Christian people has been wonderful because it reflects God's choice, and the Spirit "blowing where he wills," something that the faithful perceived and noted immediately. People, the simple of heart, are saying, "The Pope is one of us." They are not mistaken. It is impressive to see everywhere the response of joy and hope of the people who keep the faith. The response is colossal — a sign that God is at work. It is the response of men and women, children and teens, adults and seniors from all walks of life that express the common sense of faith of the People of God, the unity and communion in one faith and one love. They vibrate with joy and hope; their joy is immense.

Their applause, their songs, their tears of emotion, and their prayers are a ratification of his election, recognizing it as the work of the Holy Spirit, who is the real elector, and recognizing what the Spirit is saying to the Church: bring the Good News to the poor, heal the hearts of the afflicted, restore freedom to those who do not have it or who have lost it, heal the sick, comfort those who mourn. In short, the poor are being evangelized. All this is to cleanse the eyes of faith. This is the truth. Let us not cease to pray for Pope Francis. This is the only thing he has asked of us.

Cardinal Antonio Cañizares Llovera
Prefect of the Congregation for Divine Worship
and the Discipline of the Sacraments
March 25, 2013

# I

# CROSSING THE THRESHOLD OF FAITH

LETTER OF CARDINAL JORGE MARIO BERGOGLIO, S.J.,
ARCHBISHOP OF BUENOS AIRES,
FOR THE YEAR OF FAITH
OCTOBER 1, 2012

~

To the priests, religious, and faithful of Buenos Aires

*Dear Brothers and Sisters:*

One of the most striking experiences of these past decades has been that of encountering locked doors. Increasing insecurity has gradually led people to lock their doors, install security alarms and surveillance cameras, and to be suspicious of any stranger who comes knocking at their door.

Nevertheless, there are still places where doors remain open. The locked door is a symbol of today's world. It is something more than a mere sociological fact; it is an existential reality that is characteristic of a lifestyle — a way of confronting reality, other people, the future.

The locked door of my home — which is the intimate setting of my dreams, my hopes, my sufferings, as well as my joys — is barred to others. This applies not only to my physical home; it also applies to all that my life and my heart encompass. Fewer and fewer people are able to cross this threshold. The security of burglar-proof doors preserves the insecurity of a life that is becoming increasingly fragile and less open to the richness that is found in the life and love of other people.

The image of an open door has always been a symbol of light, friendship, joy, freedom, and trust. How badly we need to rediscover these things! The closed door is harmful to us, paralyzes us, and divides us.

We are beginning the Year of Faith, and, paradoxically, the image that the pope proposes is the image of the door — a door through which we must pass if we are to find what we need so desperately. The Church, through the voice and the heart of her pastor, Pope Benedict XVI, invites us to cross the threshold and to take a step toward a free and heartfelt decision of entering into a new life.

The phrase, "door of faith," refers to a phrase in the Acts of the Apostles: "And when they arrived, they gathered the Church together and declared all that God had done with them, and how he had opened a door of faith to the Gentiles" (14:27). God always takes the initiative and does not want anyone to be left out. God knocks at the door of our hearts: "Behold, I stand at the door and knock; if any one hears my voice and opens the door, I will come in to him and eat with him, and he with me" (Rv 3:20). Faith is a grace, a gift from God. "Only through believing, then, does faith grow and become stronger ... in a continuous crescendo, into the hands of a love that seems to grow constantly because it has its origin in God" (Pope Benedict XVI, apostolic letter *Porta Fidei*, 7).

Passing through this door implies the beginning of a lifelong journey. As we move forward in this day and age, numerous doors open up before us. Many of them are false doors: attractive yet deceitful doors that entice us to enter; doors that promise an empty and self-centered happiness that will come to an end; doors that lead to a crossroads where whatever decision we make will give rise both in the short term and in the long term to anguish and confusion; self-referential doors that lead nowhere and offer no guarantee for the future. Yet, while the doors of homes are shut, the doors of shopping malls are always open!

We enter the door of faith and cross its threshold when the word of God is proclaimed and when we let our hearts be shaped by transforming grace (see *Porta Fidei*, 1). This grace has a concrete name. That name is Jesus.

Jesus is the door (see Jn 10:9). He and he alone is, and always will be, the door. No one goes to the Father but through him (Jn 14:6). Without Christ there is no way to God. As this door, he opens the path that leads to God. As the Good Shepherd, he is the only one who looks after us at the cost of his own life.

Jesus is the door, and he knocks on our door so that we will let him cross the threshold of our lives. "Do not be afraid. Open wide the doors to Christ," Blessed John Paul II told us at the beginning of his pontificate. This means opening the doors of our hearts, like the disciples on the road to Emmaus did, asking him to stay with us so that we can pass through the door of faith, so that the Lord himself may bring us to the point where we understand our reasons for believing, and so that we can then go forth and proclaim him to others. Faith implies a decision to stay with the Lord, to live with him, and to share him with our brothers and sisters.

We give thanks to God for this opportunity to realize the value of our lives as children of God, for this journey of faith, which began in our lives with the waters of baptism, the inexhaustible and fruitful dew poured on us that makes us children of God and brothers and sisters who are members of the Church. The goal, the aim, or the objective of our journey of faith is this encounter with God, with whom we have already entered into communion. He wants to refresh us, to purify us, to raise us up, to sanctify us, and to give us the happiness that our hearts crave.

Let us give thanks to God for he has sown within the Church in our archdiocese the desire to disseminate this gift of baptism and to offer it with open arms. It is the fruit of a long journey which began with the question, "What should the Church of Buenos Aires be like?" We went through a phase of deliberation. It took root as our mission. Finally, it became an ongoing pastoral concern.

The beginning of this Year of Faith is a new call for deeper understanding of the faith we have received in our lives. Professing faith with words involves living it out in our hearts and demonstrating it through our deeds: a public witness and a public commitment. The disciple of Christ, the son or daughter of the Church, must never think that believing is a private matter. It is an important and demanding challenge for each and every day, rooted in the conviction that "he who began a good work in you will bring it to completion at the day of Jesus Christ" (Phil 1:6).

As missionary disciples, we need to ask ourselves: "What challenges does crossing the threshold hold in store for us?"

*Crossing the threshold of faith challenges us to discover that the sad reality we see around us can change.* Even though it seems today that death in its various forms prevails, that history is governed by the rule of the strongest (or the cleverest), and that hatred and ambition are the driving forces behind so much human strife, we are also utterly convinced that this sorry situation ultimately can and must change, because, "If God is for us, who is against us?" (Rom 8:31).

*Crossing the threshold of faith challenges us to have the heart of a child, who is not ashamed to still believe in the impossible.* We can still live in hope, which alone can give meaning to history and transform it. As God's children, we can ask unceasingly, pray without losing heart, and worship him so that our vision may be transfigured.

*Crossing the threshold of faith leads us to seek for each individual the same mind as Christ Jesus* (see Phil 2:5), so that each one of us may experience a new way of thinking, of communicating with and looking at each other, of respecting one another, of being together as a family, of planning our futures, of living out our love for each other and our vocation.

*Crossing the threshold of faith means trusting and acting in the power of the Holy Spirit, who is present in the Church and manifests himself in the signs of the times.* It means joining in the constant flow of life and history without succumbing to the paralyzing defeatism that views past times as better. It is an urgency to think in new ways, offer new suggestions, and create new things, kneading life with the new leaven of "sincerity and truth" (1 Cor 5:8).

*Crossing the threshold of faith means that we keep our eyes filled with wonder and do not let our hearts grow accustomed to laziness.* It means that we are able to recognize that each time a woman gives birth to a child it is yet another bet placed for life and for the future; that, when we show concern for the innocence of children, we guarantee the truth of tomorrow; and that, when we esteem an unselfish elderly person, we are performing an act of justice and embracing our own roots.

*Crossing the threshold of faith means that we work out of a sense of dignity and see service as a vocation.* It means we serve selflessly and are prepared to begin over time and time again without giving in to weariness — as if all that has been done so far were only a step on the journey toward the Kingdom, the fullness of life. It is the quiet time of waiting after the daily sowing and contemplation of the harvest that has been gathered. It is giving thanks to the Lord because he is good and asking him not to forsake the work of his hands (see Ps 138:8). *Crossing the threshold of faith demands that we struggle for freedom and peaceful coexistence.* Even though the culture around us may abandon its principles, we know with certainty that the Lord asks us "to do justice, and to love kindness, and to walk humbly" (Mi 6:8) with our God.

*Crossing the threshold of faith entails the ongoing conversion of our attitudes and the ways in which we live and relate to others.* It means that we totally reformulate them and do not patch them up or varnish them over. It means accepting the new form of life that Jesus Christ imprints on those who are touched by his hand and by his Gospel of life. It means doing something wholly new for society and for the Church, because "if any one is in Christ, he is a new creation" (see 2 Cor 5:17-21).

*Crossing the threshold of faith prompts us to forgive and know how to bring out a smile.* It means approaching those who live on the outskirts of society and calling them by name. It means caring for those who are frail and weak, supporting their trembling knees with the certainty that whatever we do for the least of our brothers and sisters we are doing for Jesus himself (see Mt 25:40).

*Crossing the threshold of faith means celebrating life.* It means letting ourselves be transformed because we have become one with Jesus at the table of the Eucharist, celebrated by the community. From there we go forth with our hands and hearts focused on working in the great plan of the Kingdom, knowing that everything else will be ours as well (see Mt 6:33).

*Crossing the threshold of faith means living in a Church where the doors are wide open.* It means living in the spirit of the Vatican Council and of Aparecida.[1] It means that we are ready to welcome others, but even more fundamentally that we are ready to go out into every street in order to fill the lives of the people of our times with the Good News.

*Crossing the threshold of faith in the Church of our archdiocese means that we are convinced of our mission to be a Church,* a Church that lives, prays, and works with an orientation to mission.

*Crossing the threshold of faith, ultimately, is accepting the newness of life in the Risen Christ.* We accept that he has been raised in our own poor flesh, to make it a sign of new life.

Meditating on all these things, let us look to Mary. May she, the Virgin Mother, accompany us as we cross the threshold of faith and bring the Holy Spirit to our Church in Buenos Aires, as she did in Nazareth, so that we may worship the Lord just as she did and go out to proclaim the marvels he has done in us.

# II

# Harmony in Education

Homily of Cardinal Jorge Mario Bergoglio, S.J.,
Archbishop of Buenos Aires,
at the Metropolitan Cathedral
on the Occasion of the Mass for Education
April 18, 2012

~

The first reading describes life among the early Christians and the point the apostle makes is simple: "Now the company of those who believed were of one heart and soul" (Acts 4:32). In short, they lived together in harmony. The early Christian communities understood that the message of Jesus, when lived in a mature way, led to a life of harmony. Although there were conflicts, they resolved them to safeguard this harmony.

Before Mass, while I was meditating on the readings, I was thinking about life in those early Christian communities and our Mass today. I wondered whether our efforts to educate our young people should follow this path that leads to harmony: harmony among all the boys and girls who have been entrusted to our care — their interior harmony and their personal harmony. To do so is the work of an artisan who, imitating God, "molds" the lives of these young people to achieve harmony. We need to rescue them of the dissonance that leads to darkness. In contrast, harmony is resplendent and clear; harmony is light. Our goal is to create harmony in hearts that are growing as we walk alongside them on the path of education.

This harmony has two key reference points. It is the balance between, first of all, certain boundaries and, second, new horizons. An education focused only on boundaries smothers kids' personalities, takes away their freedom, and undermines them as persons. You cannot educate by imposing boundaries and always repeating, "You can't," or "You cannot," or "That is not allowed," or by saying, "Do it this way!" No! This does not allow for growth, and if there is growth, it is growth that is counterproductive.

Nor can education take place with a view focused purely on horizons — shooting into the future without any point of reference. This is not harmony. Rather, it is an education that ends up confusing and distorting basic truths, and that ends up in an existential relativism which has become one of the greatest scourges afflicting kids today. When I see this relative existentialism without any reference point that assaults our kids on every front, I often think of the words of our own prophet from Buenos Aires: "Anything goes ... it's all the same ... we will run into each other in the oven," meaning we will all have problems.[2] These young people, whose lives are not limited by boundaries and who find themselves projected into the future suddenly experience problems! They will continue to have problems. And in the future, we will have men and women with problems.

These are the two things: first of all, knowing how to lead kids toward a life of harmony, and, second, knowing how to mold young hearts within boundaries yet with an eye to the future.

An educator who knows how to strike a balance between these two extremes encourages growth; an educator who maneuvers amid the tension that these two points produce is an educator who knows how to promote maturity. Moreover, maneuvering between these two elements is to trust these kids and to recognize that their human potential is great! We just need to motivate them!

We here have witnessed this. There is the olive tree that was planted in 2002, right after the Peace Tent (the International Theater Festival for Peace), which the kids planted because they were encouraged to work for peace! In 2007, these same kids worked in the City Education Project, which they themselves presented to our legislature and which was subsequently approved. They did it! They are capable!

Now, with the Neighborhood School Project, kids from state-run and privately run schools — kids of different faiths — are working together, demonstrating their creative ability and raising social awareness here in Buenos Aires. Consequently, people in other parts of the country are now requesting the Neighborhood School Project. I have mentioned three things that our youths did, but I could mention even more! They were able to do so because they were being led within certain boundaries to new horizons. This is our challenge today: to create harmony between these boundaries and these new horizons.

These young people are the ones who will care for our generation. We need to ask ourselves: How will they be when they care for us? Will they have sufficient inner harmony? Will they have a strong enough inner foundation and find sufficient hope on the horizon to care for us? Will they have wisdom to care for us like those who preceded them in life? Or will they leave us in a smelly nursing home that is more like a dumping-off place than a home for human beings? Do we know how to rescue these youths from this culture of destruction that is now so prevalent? Nowadays, when we as a nation are very sensitive — and rightly so — to any kind of colonization that threatens our sovereignty, are we also sensitive to any destructive "colonization" that alienates our youths from any harmony whatsoever and leaves them lying by the wayside after we have "used" them? Are we sensitive to this colonization driven by drugs, alcohol, and the lack of limits?

These young people are the ones who will be caring for us. We're going to pass the flag to them. The question is, How are we carrying the flag? Lifted high? And will they be able to receive it? Will they be men and women whose spirits only know a flag at half-mast and hence unable to raise it up? Or will they be confident men and women with inner harmony and a clear horizon that are able to take the flag to the top of the mast?

This is what we are going to pray for today: the grace to educate in harmony; to know how to form these young hearts so that they may live in freedom, away from any threat that would enslave them and take away this freedom.

# III

# CHRISTIANS IN APPEARANCE

HOMILY OF CARDINAL JORGE MARIO BERGOGLIO, S.J.,
ARCHBISHOP OF BUENOS AIRES,
AT THE METROPOLITAN CATHEDRAL ON THE
OCCASION OF THE FORTY-THIRD ANNIVERSARY OF
THE COMMUNITY OF SANT'EGIDIO
SEPTEMBER 24, 2011

~

*Editor's note: This homily was given at the Vigil Mass for Sunday, September 25, 2011 — the Twenty-Sixth Sunday in Ordinary Time. The Gospel reading was Matthew 21:28-32. The Community of Sant'Egidio began in Rome in 1968, in the period following the Second Vatican Council. Today, it is a movement of laypeople and has more than sixty thousand members, and is dedicated to evangelization and charity, in Italy and more than seventy-three countries throughout the world. The different communities share the same spirituality and principles which characterize the way of Sant'Egidio: prayer, communicating the Gospel, and solidarity with the poor.*

In this parable, Jesus is talking to the doctors of the law, the Pharisees, people who, to put it bluntly, believed only in themselves. They believed they were good, that they were perfect. And they judged everyone else accordingly. He is talking to people who felt that everyone else was imperfect, everyone else was a sinner.

I would like to recall another parable, another one of Jesus' stories, when he spoke about one of these Pharisees who was standing in front of the altar of the Temple saying, [in effect,] "Lord, I thank you that I am not like the other men. I do everything I'm supposed to do. I'm perfect" (see Lk 18:11-14). Jesus tells us that there was a sinner — a publican — lying in back of the Temple on the floor. The publicans were considered to be traitors to their people because they collected taxes on behalf of the Roman Empire. But the only thing this man — this publican — said over and over again was, "Lord, have mercy on me a sinner!" Referring to the publican, Jesus says this man was justified — was pardoned — rather than the other.

The same thing is happening here. We have the figure of the father, representing God, who has two sons. The first son was very good and well-mannered, saying yes to everything. But then he turned around and did whatever he wanted. The second son was more temperamental. When he became angry, he expressed his feelings. Nevertheless, his heart was open enough so that God's mercy could enter. He would then repent. This second son said, "I won't do anything." He was angry that day; he was argumentative. But then he thought about it. He thought about his responsibilities. He knew he needed to obey his father, so he did what his father wanted.

The first son said yes to his father, but then did nothing. He did not fulfill his father's wishes, but he kept up the appearance of being an obedient son. He is representative of those stuffy, neat, and tidy Christians who are well-mannered but who have bad habits:

"I'm Catholic, Father. I belong to this association and that association."

"Tell me, do you have servants in your house?"

"Yes, Father."

"Do you pay them a just wage or do you pay them below the minimum?"

"Well, Father, if you start asking those kinds of questions..."

Just by asking a simple question...

And if you keep asking, you realize that they are living a double life. Christians who are like the first son — Christian Pharisees — are those who do the most harm to God's people. For this reason, Jesus tells the people: "Do what they say, because they teach good things. But don't imitate them; don't do what they do, because they lead double lives." Jesus applies two adjectives to these people that suit them well. He repeats the first one, "hypocrites," on several occasions. "Father, I go to communion daily. I do a lot of things." And Jesus says to this person, "Hypocrite," because this person appears one way but acts another way. The second adjective is "whitewashed tombs" — those lovely, beautiful tombs inside of which we know what we'll find: rot. They are Christians only in appearance.

Jesus doesn't want us to follow a path of self-sufficiency. In order to be good Christians, we need to recognize that we are sinners. If we don't recognize we're sinners, we're not good Christians. This is the first condition. But we must be specific: "I am a sinner because of this, because of that..." This is the first condition for following Jesus. For this reason, Jesus ends with these strong words: "Truly I say to you, the tax collectors and the harlots go into the kingdom of God before you" (Mt 21:31). Jesus puts things in their proper place. He tells us that our Father in heaven is not a father who makes a pact with legalists. He is a Father of mercy.

In the opening prayer of today's Mass, we said something that might go unnoticed. We said, "Father, you show your almighty power in your mercy and forgiveness." God's power is so great that it is greater than the power he had to create the world. It is the power to forgive. But in order for him to do so, we need to make room for him. We need to open our hearts so that he can enter with his mercy and forgiveness.

So, today, as we celebrate yet another anniversary of the Community of Sant'Egidio, let us ask the Lord to always take a concern for opening up the way for those people who feel they are unworthy because it seems there's no place for them. They are his beloved. Let us ask the Lord for the grace of open hearts.

"Father, how do I know if I am a stuffy, neat, and tidy Christian, or if I am a child who wants to follow Jesus?"

One of the characteristics of those stuffy, neat, and tidy Christians — of those hypocrites and those whitewashed tombs — is that they are always criticizing others, always speaking ill of others, whether family members, neighbors, or coworkers. In the back of their minds, they are simply repeating what that Pharisee said as he stood in front of the altar: "I thank God I am not like this or like that." They are repeating the words of a famous tango that says, "Shame on you, neighbor, for wearing white after you have sinned." Yet they themselves are criticizing. That is the first characteristic of a stuffy, neat, and tidy Christian, of a hypocrite, of a Pharisee: always feeling the need to criticize others.

Let us ask Jesus now for the grace to open our hearts so that his mercy may enter. Let's say: "Yes, Lord, I am a sinner. I am a sinner because of this and because of that. Come, come and justify me before the Father." So be it!

# IV

# We Will Be Judged by Love

Homily of Cardinal Jorge Mario Bergoglio, S.J.,
Archbishop of Buenos Aires,
at the Metropolitan Cathedral on the
Occasion of the Fortieth Anniversary of the
Community of Sant'Egidio
September 6, 2008

~

*Editor's note: This homily was given at the Vigil Mass for Sunday, September 7, 2008 — the Twenty-Third Sunday in Ordinary Time. The Gospel reading was Matthew 18:15-20.*

We have just heard some words on love, but not just some rhetorical words. As the Lord indicated in the parable about who is our neighbor and in the parable about the final judgment, we will be judged by love.

This passage from the Gospel is striking because it indicates how difficult love is and how painstaking it is to establish love: "If your brother sins against you" — that is, if he does something to you — if he hurts you — go and correct him in private. If he listens to you, you have won him over. If he doesn't listen to you, seek out one or two other people so that the matter may be resolved through the testimony of two or three witnesses, with the help of these brothers. If this doesn't work, go to the community. If he still doesn't want to listen to you, treat him like a pagan: stay away from him.

What we usually hear nowadays — you only need to turn on the radio or watch television to hear it — is (condemnation) first and talk after. Insult first; we'll talk about it afterward. An attitude that says, "He who hits first, hits twice." But this is not the logic of love.

There is need for skill and diligence. Establishing love is a work of skillful craftsmanship, the work of patient people, people who do their utmost to persuade, to listen, to bring people together. This skillful work is carried out peacefully and wonderfully by creators of love. It is the task of the mediator. Sometimes we confuse the meaning of the word "mediator" with the word "intermediary." But they are not the same. A mediator is a person who, in order to bring two sides together, personally pays the price to do so. He wears himself out in the process. An intermediary is more like a retailer, a person who gives discounts to both sides in order to get his well-deserved profit.

Love places us in the role of mediator, not intermediary. And the mediator always loses, because the logic of charity is to lose everything so that unity will be achieved, so that love will win out. Moreover, the law of the Christian is the law of the mediator.

For a Christian, to make progress is not to climb the social ladder, to enjoy a good reputation, or to be well respected. For a Christian, to make progress is to serve as a mediator. Serving ... as was the condition of humility and abasement (considering oneself as nothing) that Jesus assumed. In this way, everything does indeed change.

In this passage from the Gospel (which was not chosen, but which is the passage designated for today, the Twenty-Third Sunday in Ordinary Time), in this skillful work of establishing love, I see a reflection of the work and the vocation of the Community of Sant'Egidio. These people are patient people. They are people who listen and take small steps. The words of one of the great cardinals of the Church, Cardinal [Agostino] Casaroli, might be applied to them: "These people are following the game plan, they are pursuing martyrdom through patience." They are patient martyrs. For over forty years, this patience has yielded the fruit of peace, the fruit of reconciliation, the fruit of taking the first steps toward resolving bloody wars — even tribal genocides — and establishing peace. They listen faithfully to God's word, sing his praises, and nourish themselves on the Gospel in order to be artisans of charity, of love, and of reconciliation. They do so in order to move forward, to serve as an act of patient martyrdom.

There is an anecdote from the life of Cardinal Casaroli that was a surprise to me. Every Saturday afternoon, Cardinal Casaroli used to disappear. "He's taking a rest," people would say. A young priest regularly visited a home for boys in trouble — a reform school — that had a very good chaplain who would arrive by bus with a briefcase under his arm. The chaplain would hear the boys' confessions and then would spend time playing with them. They called him Don Agostino. Nobody knew much more about him. The chaplain was Cardinal Casaroli. When [Pope] John XXIII received Cardinal Casaroli in an audience after his first diplomatic mission to the countries of Eastern Europe during the Cold War, he turned to him at the end of the meeting and said:

> "Tell me, are you still going to that place for those boys?"
>
> "Yes, Your Holiness," he replied.
>
> "I have a favor to ask you. Don't ever abandon them."

This great diplomat, whose life was so fruitful for the Church, found spiritual nourishment through charity and through penance.

One of the features of this community, which has gathered together to celebrate today, is its proximity to those on the outskirts of society, the poorest of the poor, the marginalized, the alienated. Perhaps it is because of that proximity, the same proximity that Jesus had, that the community is able to find the strength to humble itself in order to carry forth its skillful work in establishing peace, reconciliation, and love.

We thank God for this community that has gathered together to pray vespers in the Basilica of Santa Maria in Trastevere. Let us pray that Christ, with his ever-loving eyes, may preside over this basilica, where so many men and women from the Community of Sant'Egidio have gathered together. Let us pray, too, that they might continue to grow in the midst of society, emanating their loving compassion that stems from a desire to serve and a charity that takes them to the outskirts of society. We unite ourselves to them and thank God for them.

# V

# GOD LIVES IN THE CITY

OPENING REMARKS OF CARDINAL JORGE MARIO
BERGOGLIO, S.J.,
ARCHBISHOP OF BUENOS AIRES,
AT THE FIRST REGIONAL CONGRESS OF URBAN
MINISTRY IN BUENOS AIRES
AUGUST 25, 2011

~

**With the Eyes of a Believer and a Shepherd**
When I pray for the city of Buenos Aires, I am grateful for
the fact that I was born in this city. The love that flows from
such familiarity helps me to embody the universality of faith
that embraces all men and women of every city.

Today, being a citizen of a big city is a very complex
thing, since bonds of race, history, and culture are no longer
homogeneous and civil liberties are not fully shared by all its
inhabitants. Within the city there are many "noncitizens,"
"half-citizens" and "surplus citizens," either because they do
not have full rights — the excluded, the foreigners, the un-
documented, the unschooled, the elderly and the sick who
are not covered by social welfare — or because they do not
fulfill their duties. In this sense, having transcending eyes of
faith that lead to respect and love for neighbors is an aid in
"choosing" to be a citizen of a particular city and in imple-
menting attitudes and behaviors that create citizenship.

I would like to share with you a particular perspective — that of a shepherd seeking to deepen his Christian experience, that of a man who believes "God lives in the city" (*Aparecida*, 514) [Editor's note: *Aparecida* refers to the final report of the Fifth General Conference of the Latin American Bishops in Aparecida, Brazil, in 2007]. In his "Sermon on Pastors," Saint Augustine distinguishes between two different aspects of the role of a pastor. First of all, he says, we bishops are Christians. Second, he says, we bishops are leaders. Situating ourselves in today's modern city, with its diverse social landscapes, can help us in our attempt to understand this particular perspective. By doing so, we do not cease to look as shepherds upon the flock that has been entrusted to us for our care. On the contrary, we look deeper at the simple faith that takes delight in any encounter with the Lord regardless of race, culture, or religion, because only eyes of faith can discover and create a city.

**Jesus in the City**

The images in the Gospel that I like most are the ones that show people's reaction to Jesus when he meets them in the street. There is the image of Zacchaeus who, upon learning that Jesus has come into his town, wants to see him. He runs and climbs a tree to do so. Because of his faith, Zacchaeus ceases to be a disloyal, self-serving individual in service to the empire. Rather, he becomes a citizen of Jericho who builds relationships of justice and solidarity with his fellow citizens.

There is the image of Bartimaeus who, when the Lord grants him the desire of his heart — "Master, let me receive my sight" (Mk 10:51) — follows Jesus on the road. Because of his faith, Bartimaeus is no longer an outcast by the wayside. He becomes the protagonist of his own story, walking along with Jesus and the people that followed him.

There is the image of the woman with a hemorrhage, who, in the middle of a crowd that is closing in on Our Lord from every side, touches Jesus' garment, thereby attracting his respectful and loving gaze. Because of her hemorrhage, which was one of those diseases that society considered impure, this woman was the object of discrimination.

These are images of fruitful encounters. The Lord simply goes about doing good. We marvel as the hearts of these many people, though excluded by society and ignored by many, come fully alive through their contact with the Lord. This newly found life matures within them, thereby improving life in the city.

In keeping with the Gospel, *Aparecida* affirms, "Faith teaches us that God lives in the city" (514). This is a response in faith to the immense challenge that today's cities pose, leading us to a desire to "start again from the encounter with Christ" (see *Aparecida*, 12) and not from some ethical or hypothetical point of view. As I said in *The Priest and the City* (cf. J.M. Bergoglio, S.J., *The Priest in the City in Light of the Aparecida Document*, San Isidro, May 18, 2010), *Aparecida* points out a paradigm shift in the relationship between Christians and the cultures that are emerging from today's modern *mega polis*. "Christians today are no longer at the forefront of cultural production, but rather they receive its influence and impacts" (*Aparecida*, 509). Tensions that scientific analysis has set before us can cause fear and feelings of pastoral helplessness. However, the knowledge that God lives in the city fills us with confidence and hope for "'the Holy City, the New Jerusalem, coming down from heaven" (515) and infuses us with apostolic courage. Like Zacchaeus, the good news that God has come into the city energizes us and impels us to go forth into the streets.

## How *Aparecida* Envisions "Urban Ministry"

The section on Urban Ministry is a good example of *Aparecida's* effort to find an evangelical tone for examining this reality. Reading over the first five sections, we note, so to speak, an attempt at a sociological perspective. There, we observe this paradigm shift in relation to today's complex and multi-sided culture (see 509); the imposition of a new language (510); the complex socioeconomic, cultural, political, and religious transformations taking place in the urban world (511); as well as social differences and challenging dualities: tradition-modernity, globality-particularity, inclusion-exclusion, etc. (512).

Then, something funny happens. Suddenly, in the next paragraph, there is a turning point in the development of this rhetoric. In the face of all this complexity there is a breath of fresh air. Thus it expresses an appreciation for the past ("The Church originally took shape in the large cities of its time, and made use of them to spread."), and it takes note of various renewal experiences. Nonetheless, it gives the impression that these things are but little things compared to the magnitude of the changes previously described. The text of the document strives to be an invitation to joy and courage, but suddenly the phrase "*fear* of urban ministry" pops up: "tendencies to remain entrenched in the old methods and to take a defensive stance toward the new culture, and feelings of impotence vis-à-vis the great difficulties of cities" (513).

Then, the tone of the language changes dramatically and the following three points are made.

Section 514 is a short hymn of faith, somewhat like a psalm where the city shines forth as a meeting place. Let us listen to how it sounds:

> Faith teaches us that God lives in the city
> in the midst of its joys, yearnings and hopes,

and likewise in its pains and suffering.
The shadows that mark everyday life,
such as violence, poverty, individualism, and exclusion
cannot prevent us from seeking
and contemplating the God of life
also in urban environments.
Cities are places of freedom and opportunity.
In them people seek the possibility of knowing
    more people,
and interacting and coexisting with them.
Bonds of fraternity, solidarity, and universality
can be experienced in cities.
In them the human being is constantly called
    to ever journey
toward meeting the other,
coexisting with those who are different,
accepting them, and being accepted by them.

The tone has changed. So does the perspective. The question that the Pope [Benedict XVI] asked us in his inaugural address resounds: "What is reality without God?" We might pose the same question as regards the city: What is the city without God? Without an absolute reference point as its foundation (at least one that is sought after), the reality of the city is fragmented and diluted in a thousand little pieces without history or identity. Where does any examination of the city end up if it is not focused on a faith that is open to the transcendent? In order to perceive reality, we need eyes of faith, eyes of a believer. If not, reality is fragmented.

*Aparecida* took up this challenge by giving priority to a "view of reality by missionary disciples" (Part I, Chapter 1, 19-32) that became the focus for all other perspectives: "We likewise need to be consumed by missionary zeal, to bring to the heart of the culture of our time (and culture pulsates and develops in the city) that unifying and full meaning of human life that neither science, nor politics, nor economics, nor the media can provide. In Christ the Word, God's Wisdom (cf. 1 Cor 1:30), culture (and every city) can again find its center and depth, from which reality may be viewed with all its aspects together, discerning them in the light of the Gospel and granting to each its place and proper dimension" (41).

The next paragraph is a canticle of hope. Looking toward the Holy City coming down from heaven, the idea of *closeness* and *support* takes root. Our God is a God who has set up his dwelling place among us (see 515).

The last paragraph is a hymn to love, in which the Church's service is the leaven that transforms today's city, thereby making the Holy City a reality (516).

Finally, sections 517-518 contain a long list of pastoral proposals in the way of suggestions and recommendations. There has been a clear change in its tone. The first draft said, "We opt for an urban ministry," while the final wording reads, "The Fifth General Conference proposes and recommends a new urban ministry that … meets the needs of … accompanies … is a leaven…"

### Christian and Theological Imagery for the City

In a consoling tone, *Aparecida* uses word like *meeting, acompanying*, and *being a leaven* for going out into the streets of today's city. The *ad extra* pastoral consequences of these attitudes and other attitudes will emerge in the various lectures of this conference. At this point, I would like to take a step inside — in a sort of existential and spiritual retreat — and delve into the effect of these attitudes on our perspective, on our theological imagination.

If it is indeed true that we have made the transition from being a Christian people who view and shape the city "from above" to a Christian people that is now steeped in a cocktail of cultural hybridization and therefore suffering from its influences and impacts, we need to reconnect with what is specifically Christian in order to dialogue with every culture: with Christian culture, inspired by faith, whose value structure makes us feel at home; with pagan culture, whose values can be discerned with some clarity; and with the hybridized and multifaceted culture that is now developing and that requires greater discernment.

Being a people and building cities go hand in hand. Being God's people and living in God's city also go hand in hand. In this sense, theological imagery can be a leaven for social imagery.

In the Book of Exodus, in the midst of the pilgrim people that was being formed, each camp contained the seed of a city. However, the promise of a land flowing with milk and honey became a concrete reality, eschatologically, in the Book of Revelation, in the Holy City, the heavenly Jerusalem coming down from above.

The images that are revealed of *the promised city* (the promised land) and *the city as gift* (which comes down from heaven adorned as a bride) respond to and revitalize the yearnings that are always at work in any human or social imagery, that are always at work in building the city.

Moreover, the short-lived dream of Babel — the self-sufficient city that reaches to the heavens — and Babylon — the consolidated anti-city that spreads throughout the lands — give expression to (and, so to speak, help to exorcise) the fears and anxieties of man when he feels that he is taking part in the construction of the anti-city that devours all.

The most fruitful images that evangelical imagery lends to any social imagery are those images of the kingdom of heaven. Its citizens do not defend themselves with weapons (as Jesus tells Pilate). Experiencing it purely as a gift (like the treasure hidden in the middle of a field), they share its benefits with all (the branches of the tree that was a small mustard seed shelter all the birds of the sky, and the invitation to the wedding feast is extended to the poor and the outcast). Working in the vineyard imparts equal dignity to all, and relationships based on forgiving debts and on each person producing his best (parable of the talents) inspire the deepest longings of every citizen.

At this point, I am convinced that delving deeper into the evangelical imagery of the city, offering it in all its richness to today's city, is a great service we can offer. It can extend the hope we share to all those who inhabit our city and motivate a common plan of action in which charity prevails.

## Perspectives of Light and Darkness in the City

As we have seen, from the very beginning we have envisioned "that which is specifically Christian" as "leaven that is leavening the dough." This is the same as feeling as though God, who is already living in the city and is vitally involved with everyone and everything, is pressing us with urgency. Such reflection always surprises us since we are already up to our elbows in dough, already committed to various concrete situations that have occurred, involved with all kinds of people in the singular history of salvation.

Therefore, there is no room for illustrated, groundbreaking, airtight proposals that start from scratch and that allow us a certain distance in order to "think" about what would need to be done so that God might live in a city without a god. God is already living in our city, and he urges us — as we reflect — to go out to meet him, to find him, to build a close relationship with him, to accompany him in its growth, and to embody the leaven of his Word in concrete works. Our view of faith grows every time we put his Word into practice. Contemplation in enriched through action. Living as good citizens — in any city whatsoever — improves faith. From the beginning, Paul recommended that we be good citizens (see Rom 13:1). This is the instinct for the value of inculturation: fully living the human experience in any culture and in any city makes for a better Christian and bears fruit for the city (by winning hearts).

The shepherd who looks at his city in the light of faith fights against any temptation "not to look" or "not to see." This failure to look or to see, which the Lord so strongly criticizes in the Gospel, takes on many forms: the obstinate blindness of the Scribes and Pharisees; the blinding glare of "downtown lights" as the tango notes[3]; even revelation itself which tempted the apostles "holding the form of religion" (2 Tm 3:5)[4]; and the failure to look or to see of those who simply choose to "overlook."

Yet, there is an even more basic form of this failure to look or to see. It is difficult to categorize, but it is easy to describe. In some speeches or writings, a certain perspective emerges that is a kind of "leveling of the way we look or see," so to speak. From an existential point of view, the man who lives on the outskirts of life does not place any value on faith as God's gift to man so that man can see the living God and be seen by the living God. On the contrary, he sees faith as a "result," so to speak, or as "what has already been said about some topic in some document." This view of faith is placed on the same level as the view that science or the media offer. It is immediately dismissed as "outdated" when a scientific discovery reveals something new. In this perspective, speakers or writers choose a sort of middle ground to objectify traditional positions and new paradigms.

It is true that any examination or any reflection has a comparative nature, but the key point is whether there is a desire for rupture or, as Pope Benedict XVI has said when speaking of the interpretations of the Second Vatican Council, a desire for "renewal in the continuity of the one subject-Church which the Lord has given to us. She is a subject which increases in time and develops, yet always remaining the same, the one subject of the journeying People of God."[5] In terms of life, we could say that the failure to see is that of an abstract subject (that is not alive), who looks at abstract things from abstract paradigms. The perspective of faith, on the other hand, is that of a living subject — the journeying people of God, as the pope says — that is looking, from an ecclesial point of view, for living realities where God also dwells. By this I mean that those that are not looking or not seeing are not subjects, and the city, like the Church, needs the perspective of subjects (of both its ecclesial and lay citizens, whatever the case).

How can we be sure that such a perspective of faith does not lapse into the very things we are criticizing? I believe this perspective cannot be assessed a priori, but is justified by the fruit it bears. It lacks the media impact of the "hermeneutics of rupture," but it bears fruit in the long term. What fruits?

First, acts of faith increase our own faith and help it to grow. They also help us to discern and reject various temptations.

We could say that faith impels us *to go out more and more each day to meet* our neighbors who live in the city. It impels us to go to meet them because faith finds nourishment in closeness. Faith does not tolerate distance; it feels that distance blurs what it longs for. Moreover, faith wants to see in order to serve and to love, not to observe or to control. By going out into the street, faith *limits any greed of seeing with a view of dominating*; every single neighbor that it sees and desires to serve helps put in better focus the "one beloved object" who is Jesus Christ and who has become flesh. Those who say that they believe in God but "do not see" their brother are deceiving themselves.

Growing in faith in this God who lives in the city *renews hope* for new encounters. Hope delivers us from the centripetal force that leads the inhabitants of today's cities to live an isolated life amid the sprawling city, connected with it in only a virtual manner. The believer who looks with the light of hope resists the *temptation not to look*, as well as any temptation to live walled up in the bastions of his own nostalgia, or any temptation to be a snooping busybody. His gaze is not the avid gaze of a person waiting to see what will happen today in the news. The hopeful gaze is like the gaze of the merciful Father who goes out to the terrace of his house every morning and evening to see if his prodigal son is returning and, when barely visible from afar, runs to meet him and hug him.

In this sense, faith, which nourishes itself on closeness and is intolerant of any distance, finds no satisfaction in anything momentary and temporary. Therefore, in order to see well, it is involved in those processes that are characteristic of all living things. By getting involved, faith acts as a leaven. Moreover, since any life process takes time, faith *accompanies*. In this way, it saves us from the temptation of living in this accelerated time that is characteristic of postmodernism itself.

If we start from the observation that the growth of the anti-city is rooted in the failure to look or to see, that its greatest failure is not even seeing those who are excluded from society — those who are sleeping in the streets who are not seen as persons but as part of the filth and neglect of our

urban landscape, of our throwaway culture, of our culture of
demolition — growth of the human city is rooted in the gaze
of those who see others as fellow citizens. In this sense, faith
is the leaven that embraces every citizen. Thus we can speak
of "faith as service": existential service that is a witness and
that is pastoral in nature.

### A Perspective that Is Inclusive and that Is Not Relative

Am I saying that faith alone is the source of improvement for
the city? Yes, I am, in the sense that only faith frees us from
generalizations and abstractions of an erudite vantage point
whose only fruit is further erudition. Closeness, involve-
ment, and feeling as though we are the leaven that makes the
dough grow leads us to a faith that desires to improve that
which is part and parcel of our being, that which is specifically Christian. It is a faith that — in order to be able to see
others, our neighbors, *indivise et incofuse* — desires to see
Jesus. It is a faith that, in order to be inclusive, is limited and
clarified in itself.

If we place ourselves in the realm of charity, we can
say that such a perspective saves us from having to relativize
truth in order to be inclusive.

Today's city is relativistic: anything goes. At times, we
might be tempted to feel like we need to relativize the truth
so as not to discriminate, to include all people. However, this
is not the case. Our God, who lives in the city and is involved
in the everyday life of his people, does not discriminate or
relativize. His truth is found in the encounter that discovers
the faces of his people, and each face is unique. Including
people, each with their own face and name, does not imply
that we need to relativize values or justify anti-values; rather,
not to discriminate and not to relativize means having the
strength to follow the development that is in process and the

patience to be a leaven that helps it grow. The guiding truth of those who follow this development is to point the way forward rather than to judge past failures.

Love neither discriminates nor relativizes because it is merciful. And mercy creates even greater closeness — the closeness that comes from seeing faces — and, since it truly wishes to help, it seeks the truth that hurts the most — that of sin — but with the aim of finding its proper remedy. This love is both personal and communitarian. It is translated into an agenda, sets a slower pace (helping those who are sick takes time), and creates welcoming and inclusive structures — a process that also requires time.

Love neither discriminates nor relativizes because it is open to friendship. Friends accept each other as they are and tell each other the truth. It is also communitarian in nature. It impels individuals to accompany, to align themselves with, and to work next to their fellow citizens. It is the basis for social friendship and respect for differences — not only economic but also ideological. It is also the basis of all the work of volunteers. You cannot help those who are excluded without creating inclusive communities.

Love neither discriminates nor relativizes because it is creative. Gratuitous love is a leaven that stimulates and enhances everything that is good, transforming evil into good, problems into opportunities. The shepherd who looks with eyes filled with *agape* love discovers all the potential at work in the city and empathizes with this potential, adding the Gospel to it as a leaven.

These three ways in which a shepherd looks and acts are not the fruit of some pietistic description. Rather, it is the fruit of a process of discernment that comes from the object (if we may allow ourselves to speak in this way since the risen Lord is much more than an object) we contemplate and from the people whom we serve. God, living in the midst of the city, demands that we plunge deeply into the perspective that we propose.

It is not the kind of navel-gazing that comes from "look like we're looking," because the city, like a desert, is capable of producing mirages. In spite of our best intentions, it is possible for us to be mistaken. Faith always challenges us to overcome any mirage, any illusion. We have been disappointed (some of us, perhaps, too often) by the illusions of political ideologies, by viewing the city and even the entire continent from an ideological viewpoint that proposed rapid ways for achieving justice. The price we paid was violence and a growing disregard for politics — a situation that only recently has begun to reverse itself.

Today, there are other illusions. Perhaps we can discern their roots through comparison. If political illusions often demanded a fast-paced approach to action, illusions that are too overly intellectual can, on the other hand, cause delays. The point I am making here is that theory can turn out to be so complicated that, instead of encouraging apostolic outreach, it only encourages discussions about apostolic plans instead.

## Conclusion

God lives in the city, and the Church lives in the city. Our mission is not opposed to having to learn about the city — about its cultures and about its changes — at the same time that we go forth to preach the Gospel. This is the fruit of the Gospel itself, which interacts with the ground to which it falls as a seed. Not only is the modern city a challenge; so, too, is every city, every culture, every mind, and every human heart that was, that is, or that will be.

Contemplation of the Incarnation, which Saint Ignatius presents in his *Spiritual Exercises*, is a good example of the perspective we are proposing[6] — a perspective that does not get bogged down in the dualism that constantly comes and goes as a result of the various diagnoses for planning, but that is dramatically involved in the reality of the city and is committed alongside it in a plan of action. The Gospel is *kerygma*, which we accept, and which we feel a call to share. Mediation takes place as we live and as we share with each other.

Contemplating the Incarnation, Saint Ignatius has us "see" the world as the Holy Trinity "sees" the world. The perspective that Ignatius proposes is not one that ascends from time into eternity in quest of the ultimate beatific vision from which we will "deduce" an ideal temporary order. Ignatius proposes a perspective that will allow the Lord "to become incarnate once again" (*Spiritual Exercises*, 109) in the world as it is.

The three persons of the Trinity see in a way that is involved. The Trinity sees all — "all the plain or circuit of all the world, full of men" — and makes its diagnosis and pastoral plan. Seeing how men lose the fullness of life ("that all were going down to hell"), "it is determined in its eternity [Ignatius penetrates into the final and innermost desire of God's heart, his saving will to have all men live and be saved], that the Second Person should become man to save the human race" (*Spiritual Exercises*, 102). This universal perspective immediately becomes concrete. Ignatius has us consider "in particular, the house and rooms of Our Lady in the city of Nazareth, in the province of Galilee" (103).

This dynamic is the same as John's in the washing of the feet: Our Lord's lucid and all-understanding awareness (knowing that the Father had put everything into his hands) leads him to gird himself with a towel and wash the feet of his disciples. A deeper and higher vision does not lead to new insights but to humble, specific, and concrete action.

Keeping these reflections in mind, and to conclude, we can say that the gaze that the believer casts over the city can be sorted out into three specific attitudes:

1) Coming out of ourselves in order to meet others results in closeness, in an attitude of proximity. Our gaze must always be outward and characterized by closeness; it must not be self-referential but transcendent.

2) The leaven and the seed of faith result in witness. (Knowing these things and putting them into practice, you will be happy). This is the martyrdom dimension of faith.

3) The act of accompanying results in patience and in perseverance, which accompany processes without violating boundaries.

It seems to me this is how we, as men and women of faith, can serve our city.

# VI

# I Make All Things New

Homily of Cardinal Jorge Mario Bergoglio, S.J., Archbishop of Buenos Aires, at the Basilica of San Lorenzo Outside the Walls During the Mass at Which He Administered the Sacrament of Confirmation February 18, 2012

~

*Editor's note: The Basilica of Saint Lawrence Outside the Walls is in Rome. February 18, 2012, was a Saturday, at it appears this homily was delivered at the Sunday Vigil Mass as his references to the readings correspond to the Seventh Sunday in Ordinary Time: Isaiah 43:18-19;21-22;24b-35; 2 Corinthians 1:18-22; Mark 2:1-12.*

In the prayer at the beginning of this Mass, we made an appeal to God the Father: "Grant, O Lord, that we may be docile to the promptings of your Spirit." We need God's help in order to understand the voice of the Spirit, the newness of the Spirit. The Spirit is always new, always comes to renew. This is the prophecy we heard in the first reading: "I make all things new." God makes all things new; the Spirit makes all things new. Therefore, let us ask God for his help so that we may be docile to the promptings of the Spirit, to this newness.

To make all things new: The Gospel tells us the story of the paralytic who was renewed through the Spirit's power and through Jesus' power. The Spirit was in Jesus. Jesus is the one who sends us the Spirit to renew all things. Jesus is the only one who is capable of starting all over again, of starting life all over again. Consider the life of that paralytic, both his physical life and his spiritual life. First and foremost, Jesus heals his soul: "Your sins are forgiven." Jesus has the power, through the power of his Spirit, to renew hearts. We need to be confident of this. If we do not trust in Jesus' power as the only means of salvation, if we do not trust that he is the only one who can make something new, we are false Christians, we are not truly Christian.

Jesus does not force you to be a Christian. But if you say you are a Christian, you must believe that Jesus has all power — and is the only one who has the power — to renew the world, to renew your life, to renew your family, to renew the community, to renew all things. This is the message that we need to take away with us today, asking the Father to help us to be docile to the promptings of the Spirit who does this work, the Spirit of Jesus.

Today, having accepted the invitation of my friend, Fr. Giacomo, whom I love dearly and for whom we should pray because he is not feeling well … Will we pray for him? Yes or no? I don't hear you! If this is prayer, we're ready! Will we all pray for him? Yes, we will!

The invitation today is to confirm those who have come to receive the power of the Spirit of God. Believe in the power of the Spirit! It is the Spirit of Jesus. Believe in Jesus, who sends his Spirit — to you and to all of us. He sends his Spirit to renew all things. You are not false Christians, Christians only in name. You are Christians in your words, in your deeds, and in your hearts. You feel as Christians, speak as

Christians, and perform Christian deeds. But you can't do it alone. It is Jesus who will give you this Spirit, who will give you the strength to renew all things: not you, but he in you. And with these thoughts on Jesus being the only salvation, the only one who gives us grace, who gives us peace, brotherhood, who gives you salvation, let us continue the celebration of this Mass by praying the *Credo*, the profession of our faith.

# VII

# COURAGE TO PROCLAIM
# THE GOSPEL

HOMILY OF CARDINAL JORGE MARIO BERGOGLIO, S.J.,
ARCHBISHOP OF BUENOS AIRES,
ON THE OCCASION OF THE THIRTIETH ANNIVERSARY
OF THE DEATH OF THE MOST REV. ENRIQUE
ANGELELLI AT THE CATHEDRAL OF LA RIOJA,
ARGENTINA
AUGUST 4, 2006

~

*Editor's note: During the 1970s, Argentina experienced a period
of intense civil unrest, resulting in the disappearance and death
of thousands of victims. One of the victims was the Bishop of La
Rioja, the Most Rev. Enrique Angelelli. The following homily
was delivered during a Mass commemorating the thirtieth anniversary of his death.*

The first reading presents the apostle Paul's dialogue with the
Church in Thessalonica, to which he had given birth and
which he loved dearly. In our Christian life, one of the most
pleasant things is the dialogue of a shepherd with his Church,
the dialogue of a bishop with his Church. This dialogue of
the bishop with his people is entirely structured around the
growth and development of the Church. Without such a
dialogue, the Church will scatter. When this dialogue is not

adequate, the Church is disoriented. It is a dialogue of love, a dialogue of both brotherly and fatherly concern, a dialogue of grace, a dialogue of gratitude to the one Lord who has called the sheep and the shepherd to the Christian life.

It is not an easy dialogue. After being beaten and insulted in Philippi, Paul says: "We had courage in our God to declare to you the gospel of God" (1 Thes 2:2). It is a dialogue that requires boldness and courage to hear the Gospel message — courage on the part of the bishop, and courage on the part of the people. It takes courage to begin following Jesus Christ. And this courage comes from God. When you're being abused and insulted, you need endurance in order to withstand all the difficulties of everyday life, all the difficulties of preaching the Gospel. You need apostolic stamina to endure all the difficulties inflicted by those whom Paul himself describes as enemies of the cross of Christ — those people who like to be flattered and who like to be told what they like to hear; those people who want to be told what they want the Gospel to say and not what the Gospel says. For this reason, Paul says: "We never used ... words of flattery" (1 Thes 2:5).

This delightful dialogue between the Church and its Shepherd consists of these two beautiful attitudes: courage to proclaim the Gospel and endurance to overcome the difficulties that preaching the Gospel entails. Preaching the Gospel clearly stirs the waters. Throughout history, it has provoked negative attitudes among those who do not wish to hear the word of Christ. They often cast doubts on the character of the preacher himself. This happened to Jesus. They raised questions about him. They told him, "You cast out demons by the power of demons" (see Mt 12:24; Mk 3:22; Lk 11:15).

These people raise questions about anyone proclaiming the word — whether a pastor or one of the people —

through the usual methods of disinformation, defamation, and slander. This is what they did with Paul: they misrepresented him, they defamed him, and they slandered him. Paul endured all this. Likewise, the communities that followed him endured all this. They did so along with their shepherd in this loving dialogue.

It is the dialogue of the shepherd with his sheep, and the sheep know the shepherd's voice. God's holy and faithful people cannot be deceived. Someone might say to me, "Father, you're engaging in politics." No, I'm not. I'm quoting *Lumen Gentium* [Dogmatic Constitution on the Church]: God's holy and faithful people are infallible *in credendo*. When the dialogue between the shepherd — the great shepherd Christ, the pope, the bishops — and God's people as a whole is going in the same direction, there cannot be any mistake, because the Holy Spirit is present there with his assistance. But in order for God's people not to make a mistake, this dialogue has to exist, together with the loyalty and the universality of all God's faithful and holy people that transcends the boundaries of a parish, a diocese, or a country. In other words, this feel for the Gospel has to exist.

This dialogue is universal. The sheep know the voice of their shepherd and recognize who he is. They know who the shepherd is, and they know who is not. They know who is a mercenary. They know who, when the wolf comes, is going to defend them and who's going to take off. They know this. For this reason, Jesus says, "My sheep hear my voice, and I know them, and they follow me" (Jn 10:27).

He also tells them: "I told you, and you do not believe. The works that I do in my Father's name, they bear witness to me; but you do not believe, because you do not belong to my sheep" (Jn 10:25). You do not believe me because you have already taken a stance. Those who, in some way or another, turn against God's people, against those who are following the Gospel or against their shepherd, have already taken a stance in opposition to the Gospel. They interpret the Gospel in light of this stance. Like the Pharisees, they do not have hearts open to Jesus' call.

I wanted to reflect on this beautiful and charming dialogue between the shepherd and his people and the people and their shepherd because I have seen it in many places. Indeed, I have seen it here.

I came to La Rioja for the first time on a historic day, June 13, 1973, the day of the unrest in Anillaco. Five of us who were consultants in our province came with our provincial superior for several days of retreat and reflection prior to electing a new provincial. On June 14, after that day in Anillaco when the bishop, the priests, the religious, and the pastoral workers were stoned, Bishop Angelelli gave us — five Jesuits along with our provincial — a spiritual retreat in order to initiate us in the process of discerning God's will for us. They were unforgettable days, days when we were recipients of the wisdom of a shepherd in dialogue with his people. We were also able to hear intimate details about the stoning that this people and their pastor received for simply following the Gospel.

I found a Church that was being persecuted, the people together with their pastor. Two months later, on August 14, 1973, when I was provincial superior, I returned with Fr. Arrupe, the superior general of the Society of Jesus. The beating that Fr. Pucheta in San Jose, near Famatine, had endured the year before had made a deep impression on Fr. Arrupe, and he asked about La Rioja. Since he had come to Argentina for a canonical visitation — the visit a superior general makes in order to inspect his congregation — we agreed to spend a day in La Rioja.

Fr. Arrupe, Fr. DiNillo, and I traveled from Cordoba in a small aircraft. On arrival, we witnessed something very unusual. When the plane reached the end of the runway, before heading to the airport terminal, the pilot received a call instructing him to remain there. Bishop Angelelli, who had arrived by car to pick us up, told us that they had the plane stop there because the people who, two months earlier, were responsible for the stoning in La Costa, were waiting to jeer us — waiting to jeer the superior general of the Society of Jesus, who had come to visit his fellow Jesuits and, obviously, to be with the bishop, with the shepherd, and his people.

That afternoon, at the House of Culture, together with the superior general of the Company of Jesus, we had a meeting with all the pastoral workers. They recounted everything that had happened to them. I remember the last question someone asked Fr. Arrupe. A woman from La Rioja who was a real fighter, who went about God's work with true courage, asked Fr. Arrupe: "Tell us, Father. Is all this — everything you've heard — the Vatican Council, or is it not?" Fr. Arrupe replied: "Since Vatican II, this is what the Church wants."

We saw there laypeople engaged in strong and active dialogue with their shepherd. With great sensitivity, Bishop Angelelli refused to be present at that meeting so that his people could freely say whatever they wanted to say.

It is here that I experienced this dialogue between a bishop and his people, a dialogue that aims to move forward, a dialogue of love. I needed to see the extent to which this dialogue had penetrated deep into the heart of the bishop.

Bishop Angelelli loved his people to the point that, with the heart of a "frustrated poet," as we used to tease him jokingly, he was able to compose some truly loving verses about how he experienced the soul of his people: "deep and silent ravines, fiercely thirsty sands, grasslands with watch towers on the horizon, full of hidden mountains ... such is the soul of my people. The fulfillment of pious promises with the faith of a pilgrim, a tireless traveler full of memories, with a knapsack full of hope, following the rhythm of banging boxes ... such is the soul of my people."

Bishop Angelelli was in love with his people, who accompanied him along the way, who accompanied him to the outskirts, both geographically and existentially. We recall the affection with which he caressed the elderly, with which he sought out the poor and the sick, with which he cried out for justice. He was convinced that man, formed from clay, hid within himself a plan of the Holy Trinity, God's plan: "a mixture of earth and heaven, a divine and human plan that is revealed in each man and whose history forms a people" — God, the face of man, the history of a people; God, who walks alongside his people in salvation history; "the love that becomes hope amidst the people's pain because man encounters himself in every story of his people"; "that love that was made flesh in people's pain."

"Here history is a journey, and man is a work in progress." Since this man was a work in progress, he accompanied every man, every woman, every child, every elderly person, every person amongst his people in this plan so that each one might mature, so that each one might give forth his best, so that the glory of God might manifest itself in the face that God himself had formed and into which God had breathed forth his spirit.

Thus Bishop Angelelli walked alongside his people to the very end. Here you realize the quality of the dialogue that took place between the Church and its shepherd, who was also Church.

Since he was a man who lived on the edge, who went out seeking, who went out to meet, since he was deeply a man of encounter (he said, "because man encounters himself in every story of his people" — a man of encounter, a man on the edge), he could discern in that unfinished poem of April 1974 the drama that beset his country. But he perceived hope: "The country is giving birth to a child amidst blood and pain, sunsets wail, waiting for the child to be born without hatred and without bitterness, without hatred but with love, my land is fraught with life." This is how he experienced his country; this is how he wanted it to be — fraught with life: "In this night of pain, waiting for the coming dawn, with a new man, Lord."

This is the dialogue between the shepherd and his people that I discovered here in La Rioja, a dialogue that was becoming increasingly persecuted, a Church that was being persecuted, a Church that was becoming blood, a Church which was called Wenceslas, Gabriel, and Carlos — witnesses of the faith they preached, and the Church for which they gave their blood, for the people of God through the preaching of the Gospel — and which finally became blood in its shepherd. He was a witness to faith through the shedding of his blood.

I think someone was happy that day. He thought it was his victory, but rather it was the defeat of his adversaries. One of the early Christians had a beautiful expression for it: "The blood of the martyrs is the seed of the Church." The blood of these men, who gave their lives for the preaching of the Gospel, is truly a victory. Today, the Church in La Rioja, which is its depository, is clamoring for life.

The memory of Wenceslas, Carlos, Gabriel, and Bishop Enrique is not merely some capsule in time. It is a challenge that today beckons us to look at their journey: they were men who fixed their eyes on the Gospel, men who received the Gospel with freedom.

This is what our country needs today: men and women free from prejudice, free from political chicanery, free from ambition, free from ideologies, men and women of the Gospel — and only the Gospel. At most, we can add only a small comment to it, the comment which Wenceslas, Carlos, Gabriel, and Bishop Enrique added, that of our own life.

May the Lord, through the intercession of his most holy Mother, grant us today the grace of freedom that comes only from the Gospel with the comment of our own life!

So be it.

# VIII

# God Hears Us

Homily of Cardinal Jorge Mario Bergoglio, S.J.,
Archbishop of Buenos Aires,
for the Celebration of the Feast Day
of San Cayetano
August 7, 2006

~

*Editor's note: San Cayetano — Saint Cajetan in English — is
one of the most highly celebrated saints in Argentine culture.
Born in 1480 in Italy into a wealthy family, he became a priest
at the age of 33, gave away his riches to the poor, and dedicated
the rest of his life to helping the lower classes and those in need of
work. For several weeks before his feast day on August 7, millions
of pilgrims flock to his shrine in the Buenos Aires neighborhood
of Liniers to show their dedication to the saint — the patron of
labor — and ask for three things in particular: bread, work,
and peace. The wait in line to enter the shrine can last anywhere
from six to eight hours. The readings for the Mass on this feast
day include Exodus 3:7-12 and Matthew 25:31-40.*

The reading from Exodus tells us something very simple, yet
very beautiful and very comforting: God hears us. God, our
Father, hears the cry of his people — the silent cry that arises
from the endless line of people who pass in front of San Cayetano. As we approach, our Father in heaven hears the sound
of our steps and the prayer in our heart.

Our Father is attentive to the feelings that stir within us as we remember our loved ones, as we see the faith of others and their needs, as we remember both the beautiful things and the sad things that we have experienced during this year. God hears us.

He is not like the idols that have ears but do not hear. He is not like the powerful who hear only what they want to hear. He hears everything, including the complaints and the anger of his children. He not only hears; he loves to listen! He loves to give us his attention and to hear about everything that is happening to us.

This is why Jesus says to us, "Your Father knows what you need." There's no need to talk to him at length. A simple Our Father will suffice because he hears even our innermost thoughts. The Gospel tells us that not even a sparrow "will fall to the ground without your Father's will" (Mt 10:29). It could have said it just as well using the words "without the Father hearing it fall."

Today, we come here to pray for two special graces: the grace of "feeling heard" and the grace of "being ready to listen." With Jesus and San Cayetano, we want to learn to listen and to help our brothers and sisters. This is the motto that we will cherish in our hearts.

Let's listen carefully now to see how God speaks to us in sacred Scripture.

He says: "I am the God of your father.... I have seen the affliction of my people who are in Egypt, and have heard their cry because of their taskmasters. I know their sufferings" (Ex 3:6-7). Our Father hears our every cry of affliction, but he especially hears the cries of affliction that are the result of injustice, the injustice that is afflicted, so to speak, by the taskmasters of the pharaohs of this world.

There is affliction, and there is sorrow. Wages that are withheld and the lack of employment are pains that cry out to heaven. As the apostle James says, "Behold, the wages of the laborers who mowed your fields, which you kept back by fraud, cry out; and the cries of the harvesters have reached the ears of the Lord of hosts" (Jas 5:4). The affliction that is the result of injustice cries out to heaven because this is pain that can be avoided by simply being fair, by … favor to the needy, by creating jobs, by not stealing, by not lying, by not overcharging, by not taking advantage of people.

The Gospel passage on the Last Judgment also speaks to us about listening. Jesus separates the sheep from the goats and says to the sheep: "Come, O blessed of my Father, inherit the kingdom prepared for you … for I was hungry and you gave me food …" Then the righteous will ask, "Lord, when did we see you hungry … ?" And the Lord replied, "As you did it to the least of my brethren, you did it to me" (see Mt 25:34-40).

The parable of the Last Judgment is Jesus' way of telling us that God has been attentive to mankind throughout history. He has been listening every time some poor, unfortunate individual has asked him for something. He has been listening every time a beggar has begged — albeit in a low voice that could hardly be heard — and every time one of his children has asked for help.

Moreover, he will be judging us as to whether we have been attentive along with him. He will want to know if we have asked him to hear with his ears in order to know what our brothers and sisters are experiencing so we can help them, or if, on the contrary, we have deafened our ears by putting on earphones so as not to hear anybody. He listens, and when he finds people whose ears are as attentive as his and who respond righteously, he blesses those people and gives them the gift of the kingdom of heaven.

Listening is a tremendous grace, and today we have come to ask San Cayetano for this grace for our people — for all of us — so that we can learn to hear. To help people you first of all have to listen — listen to what is happening to them and to what they need. Let them talk and explain what they want. Don't just look at them. Sometimes appearances can be deceiving. Knowing how to listen is a tremendous grace. Indeed, our Father in heaven strongly recommends one thing, which is that we "listen to Jesus, his Son." That is the hope of the Father: "Listen to my Son" (see Mt 17:5; Mk 9:7; Lk 9:35). Moreover, Jesus tells us that when we listen to our brothers and sisters, we listen to him.

How can it be that there are people who say that God does not speak, that they do not understand what he wishes to say? Of course, these are the people who do not listen to the poor, the humble, to those in need. These are the people who only listen to the tiresome voices of propaganda and statistics, and who do have not ears to listen to what simple people say.

Listening is not simply hearing. Listening is being attentive. Listening is the desire to understand, to value, to respect, and to save. We must find the means to listen attentively so that each person may speak, and so that we are aware of what each person wishes to say.

The novena of San Cayetano is an example of listening. Throughout the year, we are at work asking people what most they wish to pray for this year, what most is needed. We pray and discern all the requests. This is how we arrive at the theme for the novena.

San Cayetano is, in a certain way, like the ears of our Father, listening to the special petitions of his people: their prayer for bread, and their prayer for work. The saints are like God's ears — one for each need of his people. We, too, can be saints in a sense. We, too, can be God's ears for our families, in our neighborhoods, where we move about, and where we work. We, too, can be people who listen to the needs of other, not merely to commiserate with them or to go and tell others, but rather to gather together all these needs and present them to the Lord in prayer. Many are already doing so this very day by bringing along the written requests of their families and friends and presenting them at the feet of the saint. In addition to the personal petitions with which people come, they also come with the petitions of those who could not make it here but have entrusted their petitions to them. This is the type of hearing that San Cayetano teaches us and that we are learning: a willingness to listen and to hear as the saint hears, as God our Father hears, a willingness to listen and to help, a willingness to intercede and to lend a hand.

May the Virgin Mary, our Mother, who is the beloved model both of God and his people in listening to and imparting messages of good news, receive our prayers and grant us the grace of knowing how to listen.

# IX

# FOR PEACE, BREAD, AND WORK

HOMILY OF CARDINAL JORGE MARIO BERGOGLIO, S.J.,
ARCHBISHOP OF BUENOS AIRES,
ON THE FEAST OF SAN CAYETANO
AUGUST 7, 2011

~

*Editor's note: San Cayetano — Saint Cajetan in English — is
one of the most highly celebrated saints in Argentine culture.
The reference to Luján in this homily is a reference to the Basilica of Our Lady of Luján, Argentina's leading shrine. Revered
since the seventeenth century, Our Lady of Luján is the Patron-
ess of Argentina, Uruguay, and Paraguay. The readings for the
Mass on this day were Isaiah 58:9-11 and Luke 19:1-10.*

"Together with San Cayetano, let us pray for peace, bread
and work."

According to the Gospel reading, Zacchaeus immediately came down from the tree he had climbed and joyfully
welcomed Jesus into his house.

This joy *began* as soon as Zacchaeus went out into
the street. It *grew* within him as he climbed down from the
tree. It *accompanied* him all the time he was preparing his
house. It *burst forth* when Jesus entered his house. And it *was
strengthened* when he publicly professed that he had decided
to change his life.

It all started when Zacchaeus heard that Jesus had come to Jericho. He experienced a certain joy when he thought, "It would be nice to go out and see him go by." This tiny but intense joy led him to close up shop and join the crowd in the street. We ourselves probably experienced the same feeling when we thought how nice it would be to come here to San Cayetano. We listened to that joy in our heart, and here we are — out on the streets, waiting in line, praying along with all the faithful.

Zacchaeus' joy grew the moment Jesus stopped under the tree he had climbed, looked into his eyes, and called him by name: "Zacchaeus, make haste and come down; for I must stay at your house today." Jesus was passing through the streets of Jericho, and the crowds of people that followed him were climbing over each other to see him. Zacchaeus, because he was so short, climbed a sycamore tree. He wanted to see Jesus. But when Jesus looked up and spoke to him, Zacchaeus ceased being a spectator and became the protagonist of his own story. His joy grew. We were not made to be passive spectators of events that seem foreign to us. On the contrary, each one of us was created to play the leading role in our own life.

Since this event took place in the middle of the street, this little story about Zacchaeus is similar to what we experience when we come to San Cayetano, where our encounter with Jesus begins in the street as we wait in line amidst a crowd of people, all of whom are thinking about Jesus. At some point, we feel Jesus is looking at us. He always makes us feel as though *he knows we are here*, and he promises a deeper encounter in which we will be the main character in our friendship with him. In any friendship, we always have the role of the main character.

Joy accompanied Zacchaeus as he was preparing his house. Joy filled his heart the moment Jesus entered, and Zacchaeus greeted him and invited him to sit down at his table. Imagine Zacchaeus' excitement and his smile when he saw Jesus enter! The joy he felt is the joy we feel as we wait here in line, and this joy increases as we make our way to the shrine. This joy fills us with a sense of excitement when we finally find ourselves before the image of San Cayetano, as we put our hand on the glass covering this image, look into his eyes to express our devotion, and as we look at the Child Jesus and recount all the things we carry in our heart.

When Zacchaeus felt his heart bursting with joy with the Master sitting there in his house and could contain it no more, he stood up and publicly declared that he had decided to change his life. It was a decision motivated by joy — not by any external force. Jesus did not say, "You have to change your life." He simply went to visit him at his home. That was enough for Zacchaeus to know what he had to do. It's what Jesus does in the Eucharist. He simply says to us: "I want to visit you in your heart. I ask you to receive me in the Eucharist." And that is all that is needed.

Zacchaeus' joy grew stronger after he publicly made a commitment to change his life. Zacchaeus went from accepting bribes to being a solid citizen. As the reading from Isaiah says, he stopped "the pointing of the finger, and speaking wickedness" (Is 58:9) of others and started sharing his food with the hungry and helping the needy. "Behold, Lord, the half of my goods I give to the poor; and if I have defrauded any one of anything, I restore it fourfold" (Lk 19:8). Our joy is strengthened when we put our hands to the plow, when we bear fruit, and when we "do whatever Jesus tells us to do."

The source of joy is found in these words of Jesus: "Zacchaeus, make haste and come down; for I must stay at your house today." We have a God who wants to come and stay in our homes, in our families, and in our cities.

We know that San Cayetano is one of those "homes" where Jesus "wanted to stay." Our churches are born as a result of Jesus' "visit" to each city, as a result of his desire to remain in our midst. This, for example, is the case in Luján. The basilica of Mary, our mother, was built after the Virgin Mary expressed her desire to remain there in Luján in order to be with us as the Mother of God. So it is here in San Cayetano, which is a little like Zacchaeus' house, because San Cayetano is the house of bread and work, and we could very well say that when Jesus stayed at Zacchaeus' house and changed his life, Zacchaeus became a working man. He stopped being lazy and seeking his own pleasure; he became an honest worker, a just and solid working man.

Our theme for this year is "With San Cayetano, Let Us Pray for Peace, Bread, and Work." As we enter this house, let us ask for the grace to leave it transformed as Zacchaeus himself was transformed. Let us ask for the joy of setting aside our shortcomings so that we can be converted into men and women of peace, who are bearers of peace amid the violence and aggression in our cities.

Together with San Cayetano, let us pray for the grace to set aside our own concerns so that we can be men and women who thirst for justice, who have the joy that makes us think about ways we can be more just in our relationships. Instead of thinking about what others may owe us, let's think about what we owe to others. This adds to a person's dignity: the righteous man ponders how he can be even more just. He does so without anyone forcing him. He does it for the honor and the pleasure that comes from being righteous, from giving back what is not his, from offering reparation to those whom he has cheated.

Together with San Cayetano, let us ask for the grace of finding delight in God's bread, the grace to feel the joy that comes from being in communion with Christ, the bread which, as we say during Mass on Corpus Christi, is our bond of union with him. Let us eat of that bread, lest we become separated from him and from each other. As the patron of bread, San Cayetano is patron of the unity of our homeland.

May the Lord bless all of you with joy! May you return to your homes as changed people after having fulfilled the promises you've made by visiting this shrine. May you return home with an eagerness to prepare a place in your lives for this Jesus who wants to stay in your homes!

May you return blessed, feeling a deep desire to dwell in peace with your family and with all others, with a deep desire to share the inner joy that God gives us. May the Blessed Virgin Mary and San Cayetano watch over you and increase within you the joy of meeting Jesus our Savior.

# X

# FOR LIFE

HOMILY OF CARDINAL JORGE MARIO BERGOGLIO, S.J.,
ARCHBISHOP OF BUENOS AIRES,
ON THE OCCASION OF THE MASS FOR LIFE
MARCH 25, 2011
THE FEAST OF THE ANNUNCIATION

~

Someone once told me that today is the most resplendent day of the year because today we commemorate the day when God began his journey with us. God is welcomed by Mary; Mary's womb becomes a tabernacle that is overshadowed by the Holy Spirit, covered by God's shadow. From that very moment, Mary begins a journey, a journey in which she will accompany the life she has just conceived — the life of Jesus. Like every mother expecting a child, she awaits his birth with excitement. But even before his birth, the difficulties begin. Yet, she continues on in this life full of difficulties.

At the moment she is about to give birth she has to make a journey in order to comply with the law — a Roman civil law — and she obeys. She abides by the law. There, a child is born, amid no comfort at all, yet she forges ahead. Jesus was practically born on the street ... in a stable ... in a manger.... There was no place for him, yet she remains by his side.

The immense joy she feels during the visit of the shepherds and the wise men — this universal recognition of

Jesus — is followed by the threat of death and exile. Yet, Mary accompanies him into exile. Later, she accompanies him during their return, throughout his education and his growth. She is his companion as he grows, amid difficulties and persecutions. She accompanies him to the cross. She accompanies him throughout the loneliness of that night he was tortured all night long. She's there at the foot of the cross. She accompanies her son in life and in death. Yet, in the deepest moment of loneliness, she does not lose hope. She then accompanies him to his resurrection filled with joy! But her work does not end there, because Jesus entrusts to her care the newborn Church. From that moment on, she accompanies this newborn Church, she watches over its life.

Mary is the woman who welcomes and accompanies life to the end, amid all life's difficulties and all life's joys. Mary is the woman who, in a day like today, welcomes life and accompanies it to its fullness. But her work is not over yet because she continues to accompany us in the life of the Church so that it may go forward. She is a woman of silence, of patience, who bears pain, faces difficulties, and yet knows how to rejoice deeply in the joy of her son.

Pope Benedict XVI wanted to designate this year as the Year of Life. On a day like today, when God's life began on this earth, this Year of Life has as its beginning, its most importance significance, that life which Mary brought forth and accompanied. During this Year of Life, I think we would do well to ask ourselves how we receive life, how we accompany life, because sometimes we do not realize how fragile life is. Maybe we do not adequately take into account the dangers that a person must go through from conception to death.

Therefore, the questions I would like to ask you today, looking at Mary who accompanies life, are as follows: Do we know how to embrace life — the lives of our children, our sons and daughters, as well as the lives of those who are not ours? Do we know how to give these children incentives to grow? Do we know how to set boundaries as we raise them? And those children who are not ours, those who seem to be "no one's children," do we take a concern for them as well? They are life! It's the breath of God that is within them!

Or do we worry more about taking care of our pet, which has no free will and will return what we think is love and affection merely out of instinct. At times I have thought about all the expense that goes into taking care of a pet; it could be spent on food and education for a child who does not have these things. Do we take a concern for the lives of these children as they grow? Do we worry about the company they keep? Do we take a concern to see them grow up free and mature?

Do we know how to educate our children in freedom? Are we concerned about how they spend their free time? Sometimes, when I see the programs for some of the trips that kids are offered when they graduate, I cannot help but wonder if this is caring for life or preparing the way for them to experience all the world's enticements sooner than they are ready! Are we concerned about this?

Yet, life continues to grow, and Mary continues to accompany life. Do I, like Mary, remain steadfast? How are your parents? How are your grandparents? How are your in-laws? Are you there for them? Do you care about them? Do you visit them? Sometimes it is very painful but there is no other choice than to put them in a nursing home for health reasons or family situations. But once they are there, do I set aside a Saturday or a Sunday to be with them? Do you care for that life that is fading away and that gave life to you?

In this Year of Life, the pope wants us to see the entire course of life. Mary is there, every step of the way, Mary, the one who cared for life from its very beginning and who continues to care for us as a Church as we continue our journey. The worst thing that can happen to us is to be lacking in this love that takes a concern for life. Mary is a woman of love! If there is no love, there is no room for life. Without love, there is only selfishness, and we get twisted up in our own self-love. Today, let us ask Mary for this love that cares for life! For love and courage! Some might say: "But, Father, how can we bring love to a global civilization, which amid its many contradictions seems to be set on an apocalyptic course? How can we care for life from beginning to end?" The great Pope Pius XI once said something very challenging: "It is not the negative forces of civilization that are the great problem of our time, but rather the lethargy of its good people."

Do we have the courage to set out on the path that Mary took, caring for life from its beginning to its end? Or are we lethargic? And if we are, what is causing us to fall asleep? In no way did Mary let sleep overcome her when it came to love! So, today, we ask her: "Mother, may we love in all seriousness. May we not fall asleep! Let us not seek refuge in the thousand-and-one varieties of anesthesia that this decadent civilization offers us." So be it.

# XI

# Freely You Have Received, Freely Give

Lenten Letter of Cardinal Jorge Mario
Bergoglio, S.J.,
Archbishop of Buenos Aires,
February 22, 2012

~

*Dear Brothers and Sisters:*

One of the greatest dangers we face is a feeling of complacency, of becoming desensitized to the world around us. We become so used to life and everything that comes with it that nothing surprises us — neither the good for which we give thanks nor the bad that causes us grief. I was shocked and perplexed when I asked an acquaintance how he was doing and he responded, "Pretty bad, but I'm getting used to it."

We get used to waking up each day as though this is the only way things can be. We grow accustomed to violence as something that is never missing from the news. We get used to the habitual landscape of poverty and misery as we walk the streets of our cities. We get used to youngsters shedding their blood and women picking up what others have discarded and carting it off. We get used to living in a pagan society where kids no longer know how to pray or make the Sign of the Cross.

This complacency numbs our hearts, destroying any capacity for that sense of wonder which renews our hope. We are unable to recognize evil and fight against it.

On the other hand, there are moments so powerful that they shock us out of our unhealthy complacency and set us on the brink of reality, which always challenges us a little bit more. For example, when we lose someone dear to our heart, we tend to appreciate and be grateful for what we have, for what — until a moment earlier — we had not valued enough. In the life of the disciple, Lent becomes an important time for inner reflection — a turning point — to shake our hearts out of the routine and laziness of comfort.

Lent, in order to be authentic and fruitful, far from being merely a time of observance, must be a time of conversion, of returning to the roots of our life with God. It must be a time of conversion that flows out of gratitude for all that God has given us, for all that he has accomplished and will continue to accomplish in the world, in history and in our own personal lives. Our gratitude must be like Mary's, who, in spite of all the sorrows she had to endure, did not cast down her eyes in defeat, but instead sang of the greatness of the Lord.

Thanksgiving and conversion go hand in hand. "Repent for the kingdom of God is at hand," Jesus proclaimed at the beginning of his public ministry. Only the beauty and the free gift of the Kingdom are able to enamor ours hearts and move them to true transformation — to thanksgiving and conversion — like the hearts of all those who freely received health, forgiveness, and life from the hands of Jesus.

When Jesus sent his disciples to proclaim the Kingdom, he told them, "Freely you have received, freely give" (Mt 10:8, NIV). The Lord wants his kingdom to be spread through gestures of love freely given. This is how men and women recognized the first Christians as they went about spreading the message that overflowed from them. "Freely you have received, freely give." I would like these words from the Gospel to be engraved deeply on our hearts during this Lenten season. The Church grows by attraction, by its witness, not by proselytism.

As Christians, our conversion must flow from a grateful response to the marvelous mystery of God's love, which he accomplished through the death and resurrection of his Son. This marvelous mystery is present to us in every new birth to the life of faith, in every act of forgiveness that renews us and heals us, in every Eucharist that sows within us the same sentiments as those of Christ.

During Lent, through conversion, we go back to the roots of our faith by contemplating the immeasurable gift of redemption, and we realize that everything has been freely given to us by God's own initiative. Faith is the gift of God that cannot but lead us to a gratefulness that will manifest its fruit in love.

Love shares everything it has and reveals itself in communication. There is no true faith that is not manifested in love. And love is not Christian love if it is not generous and concrete. A decidedly generous love is a sign of faith and an invitation to faith. When we care for the needs of our brothers and sisters, like the Good Samaritan did, we are proclaiming the Kingdom and making it present.

Thanksgiving, conversion, faith, generous love, and mission are key words for prayer during this time, as well as embodying them through the Lenten Gesture of Solidarity that has so edified our Church here in Buenos Aires during these past few years. I wish you a holy Lenten season. May Jesus bless you, and may the Blessed Virgin Mary protect you. And, please, I ask you to pray for me!

# XII

# *Te Deum*

Homily of Cardinal Jorge Mario Bergoglio, S.J.,
Archbishop of Buenos Aires,
During the *Te Deum* in the Cathedral of
Buenos Aires
May 25, 2012

~

*Editor's note: May 25 is observed in Argentina as a national holiday, commemorating the establishment of Argentina's first national government following the May Revolution of 1810.*

And one of the scribes came up and heard them disputing with one another, and seeing that he answered them well, asked him, "Which commandment is the first of all?" Jesus answered, "The first is, 'Hear, O Israel: The Lord our God, the Lord is one; and you shall love the Lord your God with all your heart, and with all your soul, and with all your mind, and with all your strength.' The second is this, 'You shall love your neighbor as yourself.' There is no other commandment greater than these." And the scribe said to him, "You are right, Teacher; you have truly said that he is one, and there is no other but he; and to love him with all the heart, and with all the understanding, and with all the strength, and to love one's neighbor as oneself, is much more than all whole burnt offerings and sacrifices."

And when Jesus saw that he answered wisely, he said to
him, "You are not far from the kingdom of God." And
after that no one dared to ask him any question. (Mark
12:28-34)

As we celebrate the May Revolution of 1810, we recall once again the foundation upon which our daily lives
as a family and as a society is built, and we recall, therefore,
our social and political foundation as well. Those first movements and basic agreements initiated a process — a whirl-
wind of events — that led to the eventual independence of
the nation in which we now live, and in which we want to
be active citizens.

The Gospel we have just heard draws us into a situation
of sudden but deep communion of feelings at the very moment when those who were following Jesus began to express
their many objections against him: the objections of those cur-
rently in power, those of the religious parties, and those from
a part of the crowd that was beginning to distance itself from
Jesus or that was beginning to feel indifferent toward him.

A scribe, a person, therefore, who was not very prone to
agree with the Teacher from Nazareth, approaches Jesus out
of intellectual and inquisitive curiosity to test the soundness
of his teaching. But he gets a surprise. He meets a kindred
spirit who not only knows God's justice but also has a noble
heart. He meets someone who invites him to the fullness of
life: "You are not far from the kingdom of God." By virtue
of the respect that the noble heart of Jesus shows for him,
through his simple invitation, and through his offer of the
fullness of the Kingdom, a potential enemy is transformed
into a friend. Only a nobility of heart — of a heart that
cannot stop loving as the commandment itself proclaims
which the two men are discussing — can build bridges and
relationships. Love alone is fully trustworthy. Or, to use the

words of Saint Thérèse of Lisieux, that great Doctor of Love, "Trust, and trust alone, should lead us to love."

In spite of the vagaries of history and the ambiguities of men, our forefathers of the May Revolution, despite their many differences and errors, placed their bets on the mutual trust that is the root and fruit of love, on the confidence of being able to lay the foundation for controlling our own destiny and everything we stand for as a country and a nation. True social love was demonstrated in the daily sacrifices of building this nation. Blood and labor, resignations and exile fill the pages of our history. However, opposition to any fratricidal hatred and any private ambition to hinder and delay only confirms that love, for the plan of our founding fathers was making this dream of being Argentine a reality. Inconclusive or truncated, wounded or weakened, the dream is there to continue as a reality, and the Gospel of today enlightens us and reminds us of this founding love.

It is a love that requires "all your heart and all your soul, all your mind and all your strength" because Jesus knows, as did the learned men of Israel, that whoever loves God in this way is not afraid to love others: it comes easily and naturally. Those who love with all their being, even though they might be full of weaknesses and limitations, do so free of any influence or pressure. Those who do not love with their "heart and mind" drag themselves along slowly, weighed down by their worries and fears, feeling persecuted and threatened, feeling the need to strengthen their power without stopping or weighing the consequences.

Jesus does not give only one commandment in the usual sense of the word, but rather proclaims the only way to establish a relationship and a community that is humanizing: love feely given, without any demands; a love that, out of conviction, is consistent; a love that feels and thinks about others as neighbors — that is, as oneself. Truly it is difficult to find a human being who does not feel directed toward love out of need, lack, or desire; but it is also true that our limited human condition always narrows love and turns it toward our own self-interest.

The love that Jesus proposes is free and unlimited, and this is why many consider him and his teaching sheer delusion or madness and prefer to settle for an ambiguous mediocrity without criticism and without challenge. Moreover, when their own interests are concerned, these very preachers of social and cultural mediocrity demand an ethical attitude on the part of others and on the part of civil authorities. But on what basis can an ethic be established except on the basis of the interest that "the other" or "others" awakens within me out of love as conviction and as a fundamental attitude — that is, out of this "madness" that Jesus proposes?

This "madness" of the commandment of love that Our Lord proposes, and that he defends within our being, also banishes other forms of everyday deceptive and harmful "madness" that end up impeding the realization of any plan as a nation — namely, the madness of relativism and the madness of power as a monolithic ideology.

Relativism, under the guise of respect for differences, is homogenized into transgression and demagoguery; it allows anything, because it wishes to avoid being burdened by all the inconveniences required of a mature courage to uphold values and principles. Relativism is, curiously, absolutist and totalitarian. Relativism does not allow for any differing opinion. In no way does it differ from an attitude of "shut up" or "don't get involved."

Power as a monolithic ideology is another lie. If the ideological prejudices rooted in our own certainties and fears distort the way in which we look upon others and upon society, power transformed into a monolithic ideology accentuates the narrow-minded and persecutory focus according to which "all positions are power frameworks" and "all seek dominance over others." Consequently, social trust, which, as I indicated, is the root and fruit of love, is eroded.

Jesus, however, manifested the power of love as service. No matter how much they destroy it, the power of love as service is always revived. Its source surpasses any human power. Its source is in God's loving fatherhood, an unattainable and unquestionable source. The love of one person for another is such that it cannot be manipulated or misinterpreted. Only a love that is greater, the love of God, strengthens Jesus' power.

We are invited to re-root ourselves in a sovereign love that is simple yet deep, in the love we hear about in today's Gospel, which commands us to bind Christ's love and the love of God the Father to our relationships with and to the dignity of others, whom we love "as ourselves." However, when God's name is used for purposes of violence and submission, or any other such ideological purpose, we fall into sheer idolatry and, when we do so, we are not acting in the same way as he works in us.

This national holiday is a good time to stop and reflect on "the heart, the soul, the mind, and the strength" of the love we have as citizens and the love we have for our families — on that love which teaches us to live well and to help others grow, to help others who, like us, deserve our love because they, too, are human beings, and they, too, are our countrymen. No system or ideology can in itself ensure a thorough and just political effort for the well-being of others, of us all. In order to do so, we need to seek and experience love as a precious gift that inspires ethical behavior, sacrifice, prudence, and decisive action.

Then, in light of this commandment which asks for all our strength, in light of this gift which helps to deepen our civic and political awareness, and, above all, which asks from us a noble heart, we would do well today, with genuine courage, to examine our consciences and to question ourselves specifically about a reality of everyday life that is precisely the opposite of love, that is the result of a lack of love: What leads us, through our indifference, to be accomplices of acts of neglect and contempt toward the weakest members of our society?

As a result of an insatiable greed for power, consumerism, and the misguided quest for eternal youth, the weakest among us are simply discarded like waste by a society that has become hypocritical, [individuals] absorbed in their quest to "live life like they want to love it" (as if that were possible), seeking to fulfill their unfulfilled adolescent whims. When we feel that our "ego" has been satisfied, it may seem to us that the common good of society matters little. We are scandalized when the media depicts certain social realities. But then we retreat back into our shell; nothing moves us to seek a political solution to express this highest form of charity. The weakest among us are discarded: children and the elderly.

Sometimes, it seems to me, in our relationships with children and young people, we are like adults who abandon and disregard these little ones because they reveal our bitterness and our failure to accept old age. We abandon them to the vicissitudes of the street, with the attitude of "every man for himself." We abandon them to places of entertainment where they can amuse themselves. Or we abandon them to the care of the cold and passive anonymity of modern technologies. We set aside our care for them, and we even imitate them because we do not want to accept our place as adults. We fail to understand that the commandment of love requires us to care, to set boundaries, to broaden horizons, and to give witness with our lives. And, as always, the poorest embody the most tragic aspects of social filicide: violence toward children and a failure to protect them — the trafficking, abuse, and exploitation of minors.

Furthermore, the elderly are also abandoned, and not only to the precariousness of their material well-being. They are abandoned because of our selfish inability to accept their limitations, which reflect our own limitations. They are abandoned to the numerous pitfalls that must be overcome today to survive in a civilization that does not let them be active participants, have a voice, or serve as an example, because the consumerist model dictates "only youth has any use, and only the youth can enjoy." These elderly people are the very ones who, in society as a whole, should be a fount of wisdom of our people.

How easily do consciences become numb when there is no love! This numbness is indicative of a narcosis of the spirit and of life. We deliver our lives and, much worse, the lives of our children and our young people to such magical and destructive solutions as drugs (both legal and illegal), gambling, trivial entertainment, and an inordinate concern for our bodies bordering on a fetish, all of which are entrenched in our narcissism and consumer mentality. And as for the elderly among us, who are merely disposable items according to this narcissistic consumer mentality, we simply throw them into an existential dump truck. As a result, this lack of love creates a "dump-truck culture." If it doesn't work, it's thrown away.

This exclusion, which is truly a social numbness, is reinforced, on the one hand, by the way in which the media denigrates everything that does not conform to current ideological trends, and, on the other hand, by the confusion that results from the growth of new models of family life based on "one night stands" where there is no sense of commitment and which end up producing individuals who will, in turn, bring children into this world who will continue to experience the disorientation of these adults who cannot love. They abandon them and forsake them, tragically reproducing in their offspring their own emptiness. We should not be surprised, therefore, at the rapid growth of violence against children and those who are helpless. What should alarm us, though, is our ability to look the other way, to find ways to be distracted, our cowardice.

Empty love, always vulgar and demeaning, and oftentimes cloaked in pseudo-religious terms, not only dehumanizes us, but, in the end, depoliticizes us. Love, however, impels us to care for everything we hold in common, especially the common good that is beneficial for fostering the well-being of each individual. A political policy that is devoid of any mysticism for others, that is devoid of any passion for their well-being, ends up being a rationale for some negotiating process or the devouring of everything in order to enjoy the sheer pleasure of power. Here, there is no ethical way possible simply because there is a lack of interest in others.

While I was pondering how Jesus lived out and conveyed his commandment of love, a thought came to mind. In today's world, Jesus would appear weak to many, since they thirst for unlimited power and avoid anything that conveys weakness. We cannot bear to see ourselves as weak. Any dialogue and any search for truth that leads us to work together in a common endeavor involves listening, making concessions, recognizing errors, accepting failures and mistakes. It means accepting weakness. But it seems like we always succumb to exactly the opposite: the mistakes are made by "others," and certainly occur "elsewhere." There are the crimes, the tragedies, the heavy debts we amass as the result of corruption … but "it's nobody's fault." Nobody takes responsibility for what needs to be done and has been done. It seems like an unconscious game: "It's nobody's fault" has become, in short, a reality, and perhaps we have managed to become and feel as though we are that "nobody."

As regards power, pursuing and accumulating power as some form of adrenaline is merely an artificial sensation of satisfaction that is here today but leads to self-destruction tomorrow. Real power is love: love that empowers others, love that sparks initiatives, love that no chain can hold because this love is capable of loving even on the cross or on a deathbed. It has no need of youthful beauty, recognition or approval, money or prestige. It simply flows forth and is unstoppable. When slandered or defeated, it unquestionably acquires greater recognition. The Jesus who was weak and insignificant in the eyes of politicians and the powerful of the land revolutionized the world.

The commandment of love suggests that we feel the call to work on our capacity to love. It is not merely an impulse of nature, but a gift that, through God's initiative and through our own nature, strengthens us as individuals if we nourish and cultivate it. On the other hand, without love the soul withers and hardens, it readily becomes cruel. It is no wonder that from ancient times people have traditionally adopted the term "heartless" to describe those who have no compassion or consideration for others. Love inspires nobility in the scribe and in Jesus, even though they think differently. And noblesse oblige, Jesus opens the door to building up the Kingdom; mutual trust, based on trust in a higher power, makes it easier for us not only to live together, but also to work together as a nation in building a community that will benefit us all.

Love today invites us to look beyond the short-term, taking a concern for the generations to come, and not leaving them a legacy of easy solutions. It invites us to look beyond a relativism that is immature, complacent, and cowardly. It invites us to move forward without numbing ourselves to reality, without being like ostriches burying their heads in the sand in the face of failures and mistakes. Love invites us to accept that in our very weakness is all the potential needed to reconstruct our lives, to be reconciled with each other, and to grow.

Far from being sheer sentimentality or mere impulse, love is a sublime, irreplaceable, and fundamental task that we need to propose in this day and age to a dehumanized society. I mentioned that in two of his encyclicals Pope Benedict XVI reminds us that the whole ascent of the wonderful, vitalizing force of love, of man's desire, is not complete, is not ennobled, and does not find its ultimate true meaning except in love that comes as a gift from God. Only then will we experience our efforts, our achievements, and our failures as solid and foundational, even though they may be as mixed and conflicting as were the events of May 1810. We already know where the voracious greed for power, the imposition of one's ideas as absolute, and the rejection of those who think differently will take us: to a numbness of conscience and to abandonment. Only the commandment of love, in all its simplicity — steady, humble, unassuming but firm in conviction and in commitment to others — can save us.

Mary, Our Lady of Luján, model of love, silent and patient love, will not fail to accompany us and bless us at the foot of our cross and in the light of hope.

# XIII

# God Makes Us His Children and His Brothers and Sisters, Not Members of an Agency

Homily of Cardinal Jorge Mario Bergoglio, S.J.,
Archbishop of Buenos Aires,
during the Closing Mass of the Meeting for
Urban Pastoral Care
for the Region of Buenos Aires
September 2, 2012

~

*Editor's note: The Mass readings on this day were from the Twenty-second Sunday of Ordinary Time: Deuteronomy 4:1-2,6-8; James 1:17-18,21b-22,27; Mark 7:1-8,14-15,21-23.*

Listening to God's word, I heard three things: proximity, hypocrisy, and frivolity, or worldliness.

The first reading asks, "For what great nation is there that has a god so near to it as the Lord our God is to us?" (Dt 4:7). Our God is a God who is near, a God who makes himself present to us, a God who began to walk with his people and then became one of his people in Christ Jesus so that he could be close to us.

But it was not some kind of metaphysical closeness. Rather, it was the closeness that Luke describes when Jesus goes to heal the daughter of Jairus, where people crowded around him, almost suffocating him, while a poor little old lady at the back of the crowd struggled to touch the hem of his robe. It was the closeness of the crowd that wanted to silence the blind man at the entrance to Jericho who was trying to make himself heard by crying out. It is the closeness that gave courage to ten lepers to beg him to make them clean. Jesus was into that kind of thing. Nobody wanted to lose that closeness, even the short little man who climbed the sycamore tree in order to see him.

Our God is a God who is near. Curiously, he healed, and he did good deeds. Scripture makes this clear: "He went about doing good and healing." Jesus did not proselytize; he accompanied his people. The conversions he achieved were due precisely to his approach of accompanying, teaching, and listening, so much so that his refusal to proselytize led him to say: "Will you also go away? If so, leave now; don't waste time." But Peter responded: "You have the words of eternal life. We'll stay." He is the God who is nearby, who is close to us in our flesh. He is the God who goes out to meet his people, the God who places his people in situations where they will meet him.

Through this closeness, through this journey with us, he creates a culture of encounter in which he makes us his brothers and sisters, in which he makes us his children, and not merely members of some nongovernmental agency or trainees of some multinational company. Closeness: This is what he proposes.

The second word is hypocrisy. It strikes me that Saint Mark, who is always concise and brief, devotes so much space to this episode. It is worth noting that the reading used in today's liturgy has been shortened. The episode itself is much longer. Jesus seems to show no mercy to those who make themselves distant. He seems to show no mercy to those who have taken this reality — the reality of a God who is close, a God who is walking with his people, who became man so as to be one among them and walk with them — and distilled it along with their many traditions and made it simply an idea, purely a precept, thereby alienating so many people. Indeed, Jesus will accuse these people of being proselytizers, of proselytizing. They go halfway around the world to look for someone to proselytize, and then they burden them with all their laws and precepts. They alienate people.

As regards those who were scandalized when Jesus would go and eat with sinners and tax collectors, Jesus says: "Tax collectors and prostitutes will enter before you." They [the Pharisees] were the worst of the worst at that time. Jesus couldn't stand them. They are the ones who have clericalized — to use a word that we easily understand — the Lord's Church. They burden the Church with their precepts, and I say so with great sorrow. If it seems like I'm complaining or offending, forgive me. But in our ecclesiastical region, there are priests who will not baptize the children of single mothers because they were not conceived in the sanctity of marriage.

These are the hypocrites of today. These are the ones who clericalize the Church. These are the people who drive the people of God away from salvation. But that poor girl, who could very well have sent that child back to its Maker, had the courage to bring that child into the world, and now has to wander from parish to parish seeking someone to baptize her child.

To those seeking people to proselytize, to those clerics who "clericalize" the message, Jesus points to their hearts and says, "For from within, out of the heart of man, come evil thoughts, fornication, theft, murder, adultery, coveting, wickedness, deceit, licentiousness, envy, slander, pride, foolishness" (Mk 7:21-22). Not very much in the way of praise, is it? This is how he takes leave of them — without repute. He denounces them.

Clericalizing the Church is the hypocrisy of the Pharisees. A Church that says "come in, we're going to give you all the rules and guidelines; if you don't, you're not part of us" is self-righteous.

Jesus taught us another way: that of going out — going out to give witness, going out to take a concern for brother and sisters, going out to share, going out to inquire, to become incarnate.

In response to the hypocritical agnosticism of the Pharisees, Jesus then goes out and shows himself among the people, among tax collectors and sinners.

The third word that impressed me is found at the end of [today's reading of] the Letter of James: "to keep oneself unstained from the world" (1:27). Even though self-righteousness, this "clericalism," harms us, worldliness is also one of the evils that erode our consciences as Christians. This is what Saint James says: keep yourselves unstained by the world. In his final words, after the Last Supper, Jesus asks the Father to save him from the spirit of the world. He is speaking about spiritual worldliness.

The worst thing that can happen to the Church is to fall into spiritual worldliness. Here I am quoting Cardinal Henri-Marie de Lubac: "It is worse, more disastrous than the infamous leprosy that disfigured the dearly beloved Bride at the time of the libertine popes." It is that spiritual worldliness that seeks to do what will please others, that seeks to be like everyone else; it is that bourgeois spirit of the times, to have fun, to make the most of one's status: "I am a Christian. I'm a religious brother. I'm a religious sister. I'm a priest." Keep yourselves unstained by the world, Saint James tells us. Say no to hypocrisy. Say no to hypocritical clericalism. Say no to spiritual worldliness. If you don't, you're acting more like a businessman or an entrepreneur rather than a man or woman of the Gospel.

Say yes to closeness, to walking with God's people. Say yes to tenderness, especially toward sinners and toward outcasts, knowing that God dwells among them.

May God grant us this grace of closeness that saves us from every attitude of worldliness, proselytism, and clericalism, and that brings us closer to our journey with him: our journey with God's holy, faithful people! So be it.

# XIV

# THE WELL-BEING OF THE ELDERLY

CARDINAL JORGE MARIO BERGOGLIO, S.J.,
ARCHBISHOP OF BUENOS AIRES,
ON THE FEAST OF THE PRESENTATION OF THE LORD
FEBRUARY 2, 2008

~

*Editor's note: This speech is based on the* Document of Aparecida, *the concluding document after the Fifth General Assembly of
the Conference of Bishops for Latin America and the Caribbean.
All quotations are taken from the official English translation of
the* Document of Aparecida.

The words at the beginning of the section of the *Aparecida*
document that refers to the elderly, to senior citizens, are
very comforting: old age is a good thing and not a disgrace.
Today, the image of old age as something decrepit and de-
plorable is widespread. In their ads and images, the mass media never depict old age as full of meaning. On the contrary,
the mass media make a mockery of old age, fail to appreciate
its value, and make a cult of eternal youth. The laws of many
of our countries in Latin America and the Caribbean vis-
à-vis the elderly are, in most cases, beautiful statements in
principle, but in practice what you see is a systematic exclusion of the elderly from civil life as a whole.

Neo-liberals base their arguments for excluding them on the economic burden that is involved with a growing population that can expect to live to an advanced old age and on the increased expenses and care entailed with health care for the elderly. When calculating the cost of retirement in many of our countries, benefit-sharing systems commit a real injustice by failing to perceive the contributions that these elderly people have made in the past and the meager retirement benefit that the vast majority of our elderly will receive over time.

Unfortunately, our society does not pick up on how the elderly are being excluded from society. Nursing homes are becoming more and more numerous. Overcrowding and neglect — especially neglect for their health — truly make these places "drop-off points" for the elderly. While euthanasia is prohibited in most countries, it is being carried out in a covert way through these attitudes of exclusion and neglect.

Against this background, the Church is trying to be a "voice for the voiceless." The bishops of Latin America, at their meeting in Puebla, Mexico, in 1979, referred to the situation of the elderly in Latin America in their final document, revealing the poverty in which they lived and the marginalization they experienced: "Faces of the elderly, more and more numerous each day, often marginalized by a progressive society that ignores people who do not produce" (*Puebla*, 39). It also speaks of the "total abandonment" that the elderly suffer in a world that increasingly generates more and more people who are "displaced" from the social and economic systems (see 1266). Today, the elderly are not only excluded, but are seen as "leftovers" by a society that only accepts and honors those who have power, wealth, physical beauty, and splendor of fame.

The Church proposes ways of salvation and takes care of society's "leftovers." This is what Jesus did, and this is what we want to do as his disciples and his missionaries. We want to show society, in an open dialogue that includes justice and truth, that the elderly among us are worthy of respect and not pity, that we are indebted to them, and that we owe them esteem and respect, and not merely concern. The *Document of Aparecida* echoes this situation and proposes four points to consider regarding our grandparents and elderly: 1) intergenerational dialogue (see *Aparecida*, 447); 2) respect and gratitude for the elderly (448); 3) recognition of their labors (449); 4) humane care and spiritual care for the elderly (450). These proposals are presented in a positive way: the elderly are an asset to society, to the family, and to the Church.

## Intergenerational Dialogue

The event of the presentation in the Temple (cf. Lk 2:41-50) places before us the encounter of generations: the child who is emerging into life, assuming and fulfilling the Law, and the older people, who celebrate it with the joy of the Holy Spirit. Children and the elderly build the future of peoples: children because they lead history forward, older people because they transmit on the experience and wisdom of their lives. (447)

This event, the presentation of the child Jesus in the Temple, so beautiful and full of hope, refers to an encounter — a dialogue — between elderly people and children. The blessing and praise of the old, Simeon and Anna, is intermingled with the innocence of a child and the expectations of his parents. In this encounter, Mary and Joseph are the ones who provide a bridge for this encounter between the generations. This image is very thought-provoking. Unfortunately, in many families the grandparents' opinions are ridiculed as out-of-date and lost in time. But it is also true that, among many families in Latin America and the Caribbean, the grandparents are the ones who provide for the education of their grandchildren, passing on to them faith, values, and knowledge that are rarely offered in other sectors of culture and education. This is where the witness and the wisdom of our elders becomes our people's greatest treasure: they are the repositories of the collective memory, and they know how to transmit this memory to the younger generation.

Even though they oftentimes are ignored in the short-term because of their repetitiveness, in the long-term we end up saying, "As my grandmother used to say…" If we disregard the stories and the experiences of the elderly, if we do not give due consideration to their wisdom of a lifetime, we are risking our future since a healthy society can only be built on three pillars: the memory of those older than us, the strength of youth, and the innocence of children.

**Respect and Gratitude for the Elderly**

Respect and gratitude toward older people ought to be attested to first by their own family. The Word of God challenges us in many ways to respect and value our elders and old people. Indeed, it invites us to learn from them with gratitude, and to be with them in their solitude and weakness. The statement of Jesus, "The poor you will always have with you, and whenever you wish you can do good to them" (Mk 14:7), can certainly be understood of them, because they are part of every family, people, and nation. Nevertheless, they are often forgotten and neglected by society and even by their own families. (448)

Respect and gratitude are virtuous attitudes that are fundamental for building a more just and fraternal society. Lack of respect is lack of love. It is selfishness. Gratitude is characteristic of a humble heart that recognizes that the good we possess is a gift that has been given to us. How much we owe to our senior citizens, to the elderly!

The family is the only place in society where the fundamental values that give life to new generations can be preserved. Look at the many examples of tenderness and warmth that our grandparents have provided! A welcoming gaze, a special meal, a photo, anecdotes from times past, sure and effective prayer are among the many gestures and deeds that grandparents know how to give to their grandchildren. This is why the Bible tells us: "You shall rise up before the hoary head, and honor the face of an old man, and you shall fear your God: I am the Lord" (Lv 19:32). Indeed, we want to stand before our elders with respect and gratitude and make them feel they are important in God's eyes, and that they are still useful to family and society.

**Recognition of Their Labors**

Many of our elders have spent their life for the good of their family and the community, out of their place and vocation. Many are true missionary disciples of Jesus by their witness and their works. They deserve to be recognized as sons and daughters of God, called to share the fullness of love, and to be loved in particular for the cross of their sufferings, diminished capability, or loneliness. The family must not see only the difficulties entailed in living together with them or serving them. Society cannot consider them as a weight or a burden. It is regrettable that in some countries there are no social policies to care sufficiently for older people who are retired, living on a pension, ill, or abandoned. Therefore we call for the design of just social policies in solidarity to deal with these needs. (449)

The *Document of Aparecida* goes on to describe the important role that the family plays in accompanying our seniors and our elders. The family is the place where the elderly find welcome and meaning. The Church, too, recognizes the gift that the elderly are for so many communities and parishes. Among the faithful today, they are the mainstay and the majority who attend our liturgical celebrations, who dedicate a great portion of their time to caring for the poor, who visit hospitals and nursing homes, and who are missionaries in vast areas of our continent. Their prayer has sustained the Church, and their advice has saved more than one priestly or religious vocation. Finally, through their physical and spiritual sufferings, they give us an example of strength and apostolic zeal. An example of this was the testimony of our beloved Pope John Paul II.

Even though the elderly have a place in the Church, this is not the case in civil society as a whole. Hence, it is important to encourage a policy of solidarity and fairness that integrates the elderly and does not reduce them to being mere recipients of a demographic gift. It is about building a common space for all members of society and not only building little "strongholds" where older people will not bother us.

## Humane Care and Spiritual Care for the Elderly

The Church feels committed to seek comprehensive humane care for all older people, also helping them to live the following of Christ in their current condition, and incorporating them as much as possible into its evangelizing mission. Hence, while it gives thanks for the work now being done by nuns, religious men, and volunteers, it wants to renew its pastoral structures and prepare even more agents so as to expand this important service of love. (450)

The [section on the elderly in the] *Document of Aparecida* concludes with this paragraph, a commitment to humane and spiritual care of older people, making them feel as though they are participants in Christ's mission for the salvation of mankind. Indeed, in many dioceses in Latin America and the Caribbean, and in many religious congregations, special pastoral care is being given to older people, either in the organization of parish groups to seek out and serve the needs of the elderly in a comprehensive manner, or the various ecclesial movements in which a considerable number of older people are active.

To conclude, I would refer to the encounter Jesus had with Nicodemus (see Jn 3:1-21), where Our Lord invites this Pharisee to "be born anew." Just by being born of water and the Spirit we reach our fullness as missionary disciples. Being born anew to a new life, full of meaning and hope, is a gift that the Lord offers to all of us, but in this particular case to older people. The need for companionship, a transcendent outlook that will mitigate the anxiety produced by the approach of death, feeling useful, praying, and offering up our infirmities are some of the signs of this "being born anew from on high" that the Lord is offering to our older people and to the elderly.

Our Mother, the Virgin Mary, knew what it is to grow old. May she accompany our elders! May she show us the Lord's faithfulness to everyone of every age, and may she accompany and protect us on our journey through life, from childhood to old age.

# XV

# THE SOCIAL DEBT

OPENING TALK OF CARDINAL JORGE MARIO
BERGOGLIO, S.J.,
ARCHBISHOP OF BUENOS AIRES,
AT THE SEMINAR "THE SOCIAL DEBTS OF OUR TIME"
SEPTEMBER 30, 2009

~

In this talk, I will attempt to give an overview of the Church's teaching on "social debt."

In November 2008, the bishops of Argentina stated that social debt is the greatest debt of the Argentine people. It is a challenge to us, and there is no way to postpone paying it off.[7] Thus we need to cultivate an awareness of the debt we owe to the society in which we operate. In order to do so, we need to address the Church's teaching on the subject of social debt.

Social debt is not simply an economic problem or a statistical problem. It is primarily a moral issue that affects our most essential dignity.[8] "Social debt consists of certain deprivations which greatly endanger the sustainability of life, human dignity, and opportunities that will enable people to flourish."[9]

Social debt is also an existential debt crisis as regards the meaning of life. The creation of a full meaning of life goes hand in hand with the individual's sense of having ownership over the activities that transpire in his daily life and within the social groups in which he participates. This is the origin of existential emptiness, which Durkheim observed,[10] and which refers to a separation of the individual from his social environment — a lack of sense of belonging, which disfigures his identity. "Having identity" primarily involves "belonging." Therefore, to overcome this social debt it is necessary to rebuild the fabric of society and the relationships within society.

The barometer of the UCA (*Universidad Católica Argentina*) defines social debt as the accumulation of hardships and deprivations in its different dimensions that comprise the needs of the personal and social being. In other words, it is tantamount to a violation of the right to develop a full, active, and dignified life in the context of freedom, equal opportunity, and social progress.

The *ethical foundation* upon which we are called to judge social debt as immoral, unjust, and illegitimate is rooted in our recognition as a society of the serious damage that its consequences have on life, the value of life, and, therefore, human dignity.

"*Its greatest immorality*," the Argentinean bishops say, "lies in the fact that it takes place *in a nation* that objectively is capable of avoiding or correcting this damage but, unfortunately, seems to opt for further exacerbating these inequalities."[11]

This social debt is an issue for those who have a moral or political responsibility to safeguard and promote the dignity and rights of individuals and those sectors of society whose rights are being violated.

Human rights, as the *Santo Domingo Document* states, "are violated not only by terrorism, repression, and murder, but also by the existence of extreme poverty and unjust economic structures that cause great inequalities."[12]

## Social Debt as an Anthropological Question

The fundamental principle that the *Compendium of the Social Doctrine of the Church* (CSDC) offers us in order to recognize this social debt is the inviolable dignity and rights of the individual — a dignity that we all share and that we recognize in the poor and those excluded from society.[13]

From this principle derives another principle that guides human activity. As Popes Paul VI and John Paul II tell us, man is the *foundation, cause, and end* of every political, economic, and social activity — each man, all of man, and all men.[14]

Therefore, we cannot truly respond to the challenge of eradicating poverty and exclusion if the poor remain *objects* — targets of the paternalistic and interventionist actions of the state as well as of other organizations — and are not *subjects*, where state and society create the social conditions that promote and safeguard their rights, and enable them to be builders of their own destiny.

In his encyclical *Centesimus Annus*, Blessed John Paul II warned of the need to "abandon a mentality in which the poor — as individuals and as peoples — are considered a burden, as irksome intruders trying to consume what others have produced." He goes on to say: "The poor ask for the right to share in enjoying material goods and to make good use of their capacity for work, thus creating a world that is more just and prosperous for all."[15]

In the same vein, we are called to affirm that the social question — the social debt — has become at its root an anthropological question.[16]

For, "even prior to the logic of a fair exchange of goods and the forms of justice appropriate to it, there exists something which is due to man because he is man, by reason of his lofty dignity. Inseparable from that required 'something' is the possibility to survive and, at the same time, to make an active contribution to the common good of humanity."[17]

In this sense "it is a strict duty of justice and truth not to allow fundamental human needs to remain unsatisfied, and not to allow those burdened by such needs to perish. It is also necessary to help these needy people to acquire expertise, to enter the circle of exchange, and to develop their skills in order to make the best use of their capacities and resources."[18]

## Causes of Poverty: Social Exclusion

Social exclusion affects at its very root the sense of belonging to the society in which an individual lives, for those excluded from society no longer find themselves powerless at the bottom or on the outskirts of society, but outside of society. The excluded, to whom we are in debt, are not only "exploited," but are seen as "leftovers" and "disposable."[19]

Today's culture tends to propose ways of being and living contrary to the nature and dignity of the human being. The pervasive impact of the idols of power, wealth, and ephemeral pleasure has become, more than the value of the person, the ultimate operating norm and the basic criterion in social organization.

The social and economic crisis, and the consequent increase in poverty, has its causes in policies inspired by those forms of neo-liberalism that consider profits and the laws of the market economy as absolute parameters, to the detriment of the dignity of people and nations. In this context, we reiterate the conviction that the loss of the sense of justice and the lack of respect for others have been exacerbated, and have led us to a situation of inequality.[20]

Consequently, material-, monetary-, and information-based wealth is concentrated in the hands of a few, which leads to increased inequality and exclusion.[21]

In analyzing this situation further we discover that this poverty is not something random, but rather the product of economic, social, and political situations and structures, although there are other causes of poverty as well.[22]

This poverty within our countries, as Pope John Paul II told us, has its origins and its causes in mechanisms that, imbued with materialism and not authentic humanism, produce, at the international level, a wealthier upper class at the expense of an increasingly poorer lower class.[23]

This reality demands personal conversion and profound changes in the structures that respond to the legitimate aspirations of people for true social justice.[24]

## Social Debt and Social Justice

The Second Vatican Council stated, "For excessive economic and social differences between the members of the one human family or population groups cause scandal, and militate against social justice, equity, the dignity of the human person, as well as social and international peace."[25]

Since the first half of the twentieth century, the notion of social justice has been increasingly included in the Church's reflections on its social teachings. The Church affirms that social justice constitutes a true and proper development of general justice, closely linked with social issues and its social, political, and economic aspects and, above all, the structural dimension of problems and their respective solutions (see CSDC, 201). In *Deus Caritas Est*, Pope Benedict XVI says, "Justice is both the aim and the intrinsic criterion of all politics."[26]

Social justice prohibits one class from excluding others in sharing economic benefits. It demands that "the riches that economic-social developments constantly increase ought to be so distributed among individual persons and classes so that the common advantage of all, which [Pope] Leo XIII had praised, will be safeguarded; *in other words, that the common good of all society will be kept inviolate.*"[27]

*Social justice points to the common good,* which, at present, consists mainly in the defense of human rights. According to the CSDC (see 388-398), these rights constitute an objective norm on which positive law is based and which should be recognized, respected, and promoted by the political community since they precede the state and are innate to the human person. This, with reference to the problem of social debt, points to the community dimension: "The Christian vision of political society places paramount importance on the value of community, both as a model for organizing life in society and as a style of everyday living" (CSDC, 392).

## Political and Economic Activity, Integral Development and Social Debt

Poverty requires us to be conscious of its "social and economic dimension."[28] It is, above all, a human problem. It has first names and last names, souls and faces. To become accustomed to living with those who are rejected and deprived of social equity is a serious moral failure that degrades the dignity of man and compromises social harmony and peace.[29]

There is an inverse relationship between human development and social debt. It is not a notion of development limited to its economic aspects, but one of integral development, which involves the expansion of all the person's abilities. Less development equals more social debt. Therefore, development and equity must be addressed together and not separately. When inequality becomes commonplace, or part and parcel of everyday political life, then the struggle for equality of opportunity is no longer addressed in the political sphere and is reduced to a mere struggle for survival.

Economic activity cannot solve all social problems through the simple application of commercial logic. It has to be *directed toward the pursuit of the common good*, which is the responsibility, above all, of the political community. Therefore, it must be borne in mind that grave inequalities are produced when economic action, conceived merely as an engine for the creation of wealth, is separated from political action, conceived as a means for attaining justice through redistribution.

"The Church's social doctrine holds that authentically human social relationships of friendship, solidarity, and reciprocity can also be conducted within economic activity, and not only outside it or 'after' it. The economic sphere is neither ethically neutral, nor inherently inhuman and opposed to society. It is part and parcel of human activity, and precisely because it is human it must be structured and governed in an ethical manner."[30]

In referring to the *use of capital*, Pope Paul VI invited people to seriously evaluate the damage that is done to the nation by transferring capital abroad purely for personal profit.[31] Pope John Paul II pointed out that, given certain economic conditions and the absolutely indispensable need for political stability, the decision to invest — that is, to offer people the opportunity of giving value to their own labor — is also determined by an attitude of wanting to help and trusting in Providence, which reveal the human quality of the one making the decision.

Pope Benedict XVI, in his social encyclical *Caritas in Veritate*, reiterated:

All this ... is still valid today, despite the fact that the capital market has been significantly liberalized, and modern technological thinking can suggest that investment is merely a technical act, not a human and ethical one. There is no reason to deny that a certain amount of capital can do good, if invested abroad rather than at home. Yet the requirements of justice must be safeguarded, with due consideration for the way in which the capital was generated and the harm to individuals that will result if it is not used where it was produced. What should be avoided is a speculative *use of financial resources* that yields to the temptation of seeking only short-term profit, without regard for the long-term sustainability of the enterprise, its benefit to the real economy, and attention to the advancement, in suitable and appropriate ways, of further economic initiatives in countries in need of development....

Yet it is not right to export these things merely for the sake of obtaining advantageous conditions, or worse, for purposes of exploitation, without making a real contribution to local society by helping to bring about a robust productive and social system, an essential factor for stable development.[32]

Capital also has a native country, we might say.

"In this sense, the need for an active, transparent, effective, and efficient state that promotes public policies is a new option for our poorest and most excluded brothers and sisters. Ratifying and energizing the preferential option of love for the poor (*Aparecida*, 396), which springs forth from our faith in Jesus Christ (see DI, 3; *Aparecida*, 393-394), requires that we resolve their most urgent needs while collaborating with other agencies and institutions in order to organize structures that are more just. Likewise, new structures are needed that truly promote coexistence."[33]

## Conclusion

*Social debt demands that social justice becomes a reality.* The two together are a challenge for every social agent, especially the state, political leaders, financial capital, business, agricultural and industrial executives, trade unions, churches, and other social organizations.

According to various sources, Argentineans are harboring about $150 billion abroad, and this does not take into account the dollars that are floating within the country but outside the financial system. The media also report that approximately another $2 billion flee the country each month.

The question that I ask, and that I ask you, is as follows: What can we do so that these resources are put to the service of the country in order to address the social debt and create conditions for an integral development for everyone?

In our case, social debt is the millions of Argentineans, mostly children and young people, who demand from us an *ethical, cultural response of solidarity.* This obliges us to work to change the structural causes as well as the personal and corporate attitudes that create this situation, and, through dialogue, to reach agreements that will permit us to transform this painful reality of social debt.

The Church, in recognizing and speaking about the social debt, manifests once more its preferential love for the poor and marginalized,[34] with whom Jesus especially identified himself (see Mt 25:40). It does so "in the light of the primacy of charity, which is attested to throughout Christian tradition, beginning with that of the early Church (see Acts 4:32; 1 Cor 16:1; 2 Cor 8-9; Gal 2:10),"[35] and in accordance with the prophetic tradition (see Is 1:11-17; Jer 7:4-7; Am 5:21-25).

It is essential for the Church to address the problem of social debt because mankind, and especially the poor, is precisely the path of the Church because this was the path of Jesus Christ.

# XVI

# Priests, Religious, and Laity

## Lenten Letter of Cardinal Jorge Mario Bergoglio, S.J., Archbishop of Buenos Aires, February 13, 2013

~

*"'[Rend] your hearts and not your garments.' Return to the Lord, your God, for he is gracious and merciful, slow to anger, and abounding in mercy" (Jl 2:13).*

Little by little, we have grown accustomed to hearing and seeing a rather dismal chronicle of contemporary society that the mass media presents to us with an almost perverse sense of elation. Moreover, we have grown accustomed to its influence all around us — even in our own flesh. This drama is being played out in our streets, in our neighborhoods, in our homes, and even in our own hearts.

Together we experience the violence that kills, destroys families, fuels wars and conflicts in so many countries of the world. Together we experience envy, hatred, slander, and worldliness in our own hearts. The suffering of innocent and peace-loving people never ceases to buffet us; contempt for the rights of the most vulnerable individuals and nations is never far away from us; the tyrannical rule of money with its demonic effects, such as drugs, corruption, and human trafficking — including children — along with material and moral misery are now common currency. The destruction of the dignity of work, the pain of emigration, and the lack of a future are also part of this tragic symphony.

Our errors and sins as a Church are also a part of the sad panorama. We rationalize our own selfishness — and not just the subtlest forms of it — as well as the lack of ethical values within society that is spreading quickly in our families and in our life together in our neighborhoods, towns, and cities, which testify to our limitations, our weaknesses, and our inability to transform this endless list of destructive realities.

Trapped in our powerlessness, we cannot help but wonder: Does it make any sense to try to change all this? Can we do anything about this? Is it even worthwhile to try to do so if the world persists in its carnival-like dance in an effort to disguise all this even for a little while? Nevertheless, when the mask falls off and the truth appears, even though to many it may sound old-fashioned to say so, sin once again will appear, wounding our very flesh with all its destructive force, altering the destinies of the world and of history.

Lent comes to us with its shout of truth and hope. It tells us that we do not have to slap on makeup and draw plastic smiles as if nothing were happening. Yes, it is possible for all things to be made new and different, because God remains *rich in kindness and mercy, unrelenting in forgiveness,* and encourages us repeatedly to begin anew. Today, once again, God invites us to begin our paschal journey toward life, a journey that includes the cross and self-denial, a journey that may be uncomfortable but not fruitless. He invites us to admit that something inside us is not well, and that something in society or in the Church is not well. He invites us to change, to turn around, and to be converted.

Today, the words of the prophet Joel are strong and challenging: *Rend your hearts, and not your garments, and return to the Lord your God.* These words are an invitation to all people; they exclude no one.

*Rend your hearts and your garments* of a penance that is not sincere and that does not guarantee an eternal future.

*Rend your hearts and not your garments* of any fast that is merely a formality or an observance, which only serves to make us feel satisfied.

*Rend your hearts and not your garments* of superficial and self-centered prayer that does not reach the innermost being of your life so that God may touch it.

*Rend your hearts* so that you may say along with the psalmist, "We have sinned" (see Ps 106:6). As St. Gregory the Great says,

> The wound of the soul is sin: Oh, poor wounded one, recognize your physician! Show him the wounds of your faults. Since we cannot hide from him our most secret thoughts, make him hear the cry of your heart. Move him to compassion with your tears, with your insistence beg him! Let him hear your sighs that your pain may reach him, so that, at the end, he can say to you, "The Lord has forgiven your sin."

This is the reality of our human condition. This truth can bring us to authentic reconciliation with God and with other men and women. This is not a matter of damaging our self-esteem. Rather, we are penetrating to the depths of our heart and taking on the mystery of suffering and pain, which has bound us for centuries, for thousands of years, forever.

*Rend your hearts* so that through this cleft we will truly be able to see ourselves as we are.

*Rend your hearts*, open your hearts, because the merciful love of the Father who loves us and heals us can only enter into hearts that have been broken.

*Rend your hearts*, the prophet says, and Paul begs us, almost on his knees, to "be reconciled to God" (2 Cor 5:20). Changing our way of living is both a sign and the fruit of a heart that has been broken and reconciled by a love that overwhelms us. This is God's invitation to us in the face of the many wounds that have harmed us and can lure us to the temptation to harden our hearts.

*Rend your hearts* so you can experience God's gentle tenderness in the serenity and silence of prayer.

*Rend your hearts* to hear the sound of so many lives torn apart, lest our indifference leave us numb.

*Rend your hearts* so that you will be able to love with the love with which we are loved, to console with the consolation that consoles us, and to share what we have received.

The liturgical season that the Church begins today is not only for us, but also for the transformation of our families, our communities, our Church, our country — of the whole world. These are forty days during which we may experience conversion to God's own holiness. These are forty days during which we may become his co-workers who receive the grace and the potential to reconstruct human life so that everyone may experience the salvation that Christ won for us by his death and resurrection.

Together with prayer and penance, as a sign of our faith in Easter's power to transform all things, we also begin, as in previous years, our "Lenten Gesture of Solidarity." As the Church here in Buenos Aires — that is on its journey toward Easter and that believes that the kingdom of God is indeed possible — we need grace to be poured forth in hearts that are broken open by a desire for conversion and by love. We need effective gestures that will alleviate the pain of so many of our brothers and sisters who walk alongside us. "No act of virtue can be great if it does not also benefit others.... Therefore, no matter how much you fast, no matter how much you sleep on a hard floor, eat ashes, and sigh continuously, if you do not do good to others, you do not accomplish anything great" (St. John Chrysostom).

This Year of Faith, which we are now experiencing, is also an opportunity that God is giving us to grow and mature in our encounter with the Lord. He becomes visible to us in the suffering faces of so many children without a future, in the trembling hands of the forsaken elderly, and in the wobbly knees of so many families who continue to face life without any support.

I wish you a holy Lent, a penitential and fruitful Lent, and, please, I ask you all to pray for me. May Jesus bless you, and may the Blessed Virgin Mary protect you.

# XVII

# Children and Youth Living in the Streets

Message by Cardinal Jorge Mario
Bergoglio, S.J.,
Archbishop of Buenos Aires,
in honor of the Feast of St. Thérèse
of the Child Jesus
October 1, 2005

~

*Dear Brothers and Sisters:*

The motto for the Thirty-first Youth Pilgrimage to the Shrine of Our Lady of Luján is "Mother, Help Us to Care for Life." We are asking our Mother for the grace to care for all life and all of life. We do so in the filial cry of prayer and trust that Our Lady gives to us. Our Lady said to Juan Diego, "Am I not here, who is your mother?" Knowing that she is nearby with her motherly care gives us strength to ask her with the heart of a child, "Mother, help us to care for life." In light of our filial prayer, I would like to bring to your attention a problem regarding life that affects our city.

In the last few years, we have seen some new realities emerge in our cities: blockaded streets, picket lines, people living by the side of the road. In my opinion, the latter is the most painful, because the victims are children. These unjust and dangerous situations, whose victims are our little boys, little girls, and adolescents, both shock us and upset us.

We encounter children and young people living in the streets, begging, sleeping in subway and railroad stations, doorways, and porticoes — either alone or in groups — simply "hoping." These are daily realities in our city.

We see children and young people picking up cardboard boxes and going through the trash — even into the night — seeking to find the only meal they might have that day.

We see children and young people, many times working under the watchful eye of adults who take advantage of them, busy doing a variety of formal or informal jobs, as vendors, as jugglers, cleaning windows, opening car doors, and selling stamps in the subway to make a few cents.

In the city of Buenos Aires, a person can be arrested or fined if he uses an animal, like a horse, to pull a cart through the streets. Yet, every day in the neighborhood known as the Microcentro, I see hundreds of carts loaded with cardboard or paper being pushed by kids because their owners cannot use a horse to transport their goods! Are our kids less valuable than animals?

On August 13, we read in the newspapers about a pedophilia ring that was operating in various sections of town: Chacaritas, Floresta, Congreso, Recoleta, San Telmo, Monserrat, Nuñez, Palermo y Caballito. Children between the ages of five and fifteen were having sexual relationships with adults! A few years ago, we were rending our garments when we found out that "sex tours" to certain places in Asia, which included sex with children, were being organized in Europe. Now we have them right here in our city. They are even included on the list of activities at some of our most luxurious hotels!

Another painful reality is the growing use of children and teens for drug trafficking. The massive use of alcohol among children and young people, made possible by the complicity of unscrupulous storeowners, is yet another aberration, to the point that we even see very young children who are now prone to drinking.

On the other hand, statistics show that most of our children are poor and that fifty percent of our poor are children. Such levels of destitution dramatically affect the current reality as well as our very near future reality, and we can already see their consequences, including a lack of nutrition, environmental pollution, unhealthy living conditions and disease, violence and promiscuity. All of these have an effect on their growth. They cause problems in their personal relationships. Their integration into the community and into society becomes a challenge. One of the most chilling developments recently is the fact that tour operators now include visits to the emergency shelters where destitute and poor children live as part of the tours they offer to foreign visitors.

As many prestigious institutions and personalities have pointed out, cultural productions, especially television, offer our children and young people a constant fare of programming where sexuality is trivialized and degraded, where family life is devalued, where vice is artificially depicted as virtue, and where violence and irresponsible freedom are exalted. The result is a paradigm shift in the behavior of our young people, aided by the passivity of watchdog agencies and the complicity of businesses and institutions that have a financial stake in them.

This reality conveys a moral degradation that continues to grow and deepen, and that leads us to ask ourselves: How can we recover a respect for the life and dignity of our children? We are robbing so many of them of their childhood and their future — as well as of our future. As a society, we share this responsibility. However, it weighs more heavily on those of us who possess greater power, education, and wealth.

When we look at the spiritual reality, we see that many children do not even know how to pray! We see that many children have never been taught how to look for and gaze upon the face of the Father in heaven who loves them and treasures them. This is a grave loss at the core of their being.

All of these realities shake us up and force us to face our responsibility as Christians, our obligation as citizens, and our solidarity as part of a community that, with each passing day, we hope will be more humane, more worthy, and more capable of recognizing the dignity of the human being and of society as a whole.

The realities our children and young people face elicit various reactions. On one hand, there is a gradual complacency as the result of growing passivity and indifference, as well as some sort of "normality" vis-à-vis the injustices. On the other hand, there is an attitude that, mistakenly, is becoming the norm and is, therefore, becoming rather commonplace. It calls for repressive measures and growing control that extend from lowering the age of criminal responsibility to the forced separation of families. At times, the judicial system unjustly forces poor families to submit to a discretional and even abusive institutionalization of their children.

The description can go on and on, but it requires an outcry from us — a cry for awareness. We need to be aware that the situation of our children and young people is critical. We need to own up to our responsibilities — as individuals and as a society — for this critical situation. We need to assume our responsibilities, as laid out in our constitution, in this regard.

We need to realize that every child who is an outcast, who is abandoned, who is left out on the street — without the benefit of an education and without adequate health care — is the full expression not only of an injustice but also of a breakdown in our institutions. This includes the family and the institutions that surround it: neighborhood associations, parishes, the various government agencies. Many of these situations require an immediate response — but not just through some flashy outburst. In the quest for permanent solutions and their subsequent implementation, we cannot forget that we need a change of heart and mindset that will move us to give value and dignity to the life of these children — from the moment they are conceived in their mother's womb to the moment they find rest in the bosom of God the Father — and that will move us to work each day to ensure this will happen.

We need to enter into God's heart to begin to listen to the voice of the weakest among us — these children and these young people. We need to recall Our Lord's words to us: "Whoever receives one such child in my name receives me" (Mt 18:5). Let us also recall these words: "See that you do not despise one of these little ones; for I tell you that in heaven their angels always behold the face of my Father who is in heaven" (Mt 18:10). Their voices, as well as the Lord's words to us, should move us to make a commitment to action:

- No child will be left abandoned in our cities.
- No young person or teen will be left destitute in our cities.
- No Christian, no parish, and no civil authority should remain apathetic or indifferent to the hardships that our children and our families face.

- No selfish interest, either personal or collective, should interfere or slow down our force or commitment to the urgent need to coordinate and work together to make an immediate and pressing change.

I am concerned about this situation, which pains me. For this reason, I have written this letter. I have brought up this issue with some specialists, like the Episcopal Vicariate for Children, the Commission for Children and Teens at Risk, as well as various civil judges and legislators. Above all, though, I want to make sure that we do not grow accustomed to this new reality within our city where the victims are children. I beg you: Please open your hearts to this painful reality. The Herods of today wear many different masks, but the truth is the same: they kill children; they kill their smiles; they kill their hope. The flesh of our children is not cannon fodder.

Let us look with renewed eyes at the children in our cities, and let us be brave enough to weep together. Let us look at Our Lady and plead with the tears of our hearts: "Mother, help us to care for life."

# XVIII

# MARRIAGE

OPEN LETTER TO MR. JUSTO CARBAJALES,
DIRECTOR OF THE DEPARTMENT FOR THE LAITY OF
THE ARGENTINEAN BISHOPS' CONFERENCE,
FROM CARDINAL JORGE MARIO BERGOGLIO, S.J.,
ARCHBISHOP OF BUENOS AIRES
JULY 27, 2010

~

*Dear Justo:*

The members of the Department for the Laity of the Argentinean Bishops' Conference, in their role as private citizens, have undertaken an initiative to organize a demonstration against the possible enactment of a law legalizing same-sex marriage. At the same time, they reaffirmed the need to ensure the right of children to have a father and a mother for their upbringing and education. I am writing this letter because I wish to show my support for this expression of responsibility on the part of the laity.

I know, because you have told me, that this act is not directed against anyone in particular, because our intent is not to judge those who think or feel differently than we do. However, in these times more than ever, as we prepare to celebrate our bicentennial as a nation that includes the assurance of the plurality and diversity of its citizens, we clearly maintain that it is not possible to make equal what is diverse;

in our coexistence as a society the acceptance of differences is necessary. This is not merely a question of terminology or formal conventions of a private relationship. Rather, it is a natural anthropological bond. The human being, in his very essence, tends to this union of a man and a woman for mutual fulfillment, attention and care, as well as the natural way for procreation. This confers an importance upon marriage, both socially and politically. Marriage precedes the state: it is the foundation for the family and for a cell within society, predating any legislation, and even predating the Church itself. Therefore, the approval of a law in favor of same-sex marriage would mean a very real and grave step backward from an anthropological point of view.

Marriage between a man and a woman is not the same as a union between two people of the same gender. To make a distinction is not to discriminate but to respect; to differentiate in order to discern is to properly assess, not to discriminate. In a time when we place so much emphasis on the value of pluralism and cultural and social diversity, it is actually a contradiction to minimize our fundamental human differences. A father is not the same as a mother. We cannot teach future generations that the task of raising a family in a stable, committed relationship between a man and a woman is the same as two people of the same sex living together.

In this effort to ensure and safeguard an alleged right for adults, let us take care not to ignore the overriding right of children (who should be the only privileged members of society) to have a mother and a father as their models, to have a mom and a dad.

For your part, I ask you to take care, in your speech and in your heart, not to show any aggression or violence toward any brother or sister. As Christians, we should behave as servants of the truth, not as owners of the truth. I pray that Our Lord, in his meekness, the meekness that he asks from all of us, may accompany you in all you do.

I ask that you pray for me, and that you ask others to pray for me. May Jesus bless you, and may the Virgin Mary protect you.

Your brother in Christ,

Cardinal Jorge Mario Bergoglio, S.J.

Archbishop of Buenos Aires

# XIX

# PRAYER

A LETTER TO PRIESTS AND RELIGIOUS OF THE
ARCHDIOCESE OF BUENOS AIRES
BY CARDINAL JORGE MARIO BERGOGLIO, S.J.,
ARCHBISHOP OF BUENOS AIRES.
JULY 29, 2007

~

*Editor's note: This letter was inspired by the readings for Sunday, July 29, 2007 — the Seventeenth Sunday in Ordinary Time: Genesis 18:20-32; Colossians 2:12-14; and Luke 11:1-13.*

*Dear Brothers and Sisters:*

I felt prompted to write this letter to you after meditating on the readings for this Sunday. I'm not sure why, but I felt strongly that I should do so. It began as a question: Do I pray? It then led to another question: Do we, the priests and religious of the archdiocese, pray? Do we pray enough? Do we pray as much as we should? I first had to answer the question myself. In asking you this question, my desire is that each one of you can sincerely answer it.

The sheer number and severity of the problems we face each day move us to action — to find solutions, to come up with new ways, to build. This occupies a large part of our day. We are hardworking laborers in the Kingdom and, at the end of the day, we find ourselves tired out due to all our activity. I believe we can honestly say that we are not slackers. We always have work to do here in the archdiocese. The constant demands and the urgent need for our services begin to wear on us, and we end up consumed by our service to Our Lord and to his Church.

On the other hand, we also feel the weight, and not without anguish, of the pagan civilization that surrounds us. It publically proclaims its principles and so-called values in such an audacious and self-assured way that we find ourselves wavering in our own convictions, in our apostolic endurance, and even in our faith in the Lord — in the Lord whom we know is alive and is at work in human history and in his Church. At the end of the day, we sometimes feel depleted and, without realizing it, pessimism sets in. In defeat, we retreat, cowardly, and become defensive. Consequently, our souls are scarred and we become overly cautious.

Thus, in the midst of this intense and exhausting apostolic work on one hand and a very aggressive pagan culture on the other, our hearts shrink back because we feel powerless. We adopt a minimalist attitude just trying to survive as we attempt to preserve our faith. However, we are not stupid; we know something is missing. What was meant to be a new horizon has now become a fence, limiting our apostolic zeal to proclaim the Kingdom. Could it be that we try to do everything by ourselves, thus losing our focus and feeling responsible for coming up with all the solutions? We know that we cannot do it alone. Here is the question: Do we give time and space to Our Lord during the day so he can do his work, or are we so busy doing everything by ourselves that we do not let him enter?

I imagine Abraham was very scared when God told him that he was going to destroy Sodom. He thought about his relatives, of course, and he even took a step further: Was there any possibility of saving those poor people? Thus the bargaining began. In spite of the holy sense of fear that he experienced in the presence of the Lord, Abraham felt responsible. He was not at peace asking just once. He felt that he should intercede in order to save the situation. He felt he needed to wrestle with God. He was no longer thinking merely of his relatives, but of the whole town ... and he intercedes even more (see Gn 18:16-32). He goes hand in hand with God. He could have relaxed with a clean conscience after his first attempt, rejoicing in the promise of a son that the Lord had just made (Gn 18:9). Instead, he continues to wrestle with God. Unconsciously, perhaps, he might have felt that the sinful people in the town were like his own son. I am not sure. Nonetheless, he decides to gamble. Courageously he intercedes, but he is also taking the risk of angering God. It is the courage of true intercession.

On several occasions, I have spoken about boldness, courage, and fervor in our apostolic work. We must have the same attitude in our prayer: we must pray with *parresia* — with courage, boldness, and confidence. We cannot sit still after having prayed once. True Christian intercession consists of insisting to the very end.

This is how David prayed when he prayed for his dying son (see 2 Sm 12:15-18). This is how Moses prayed for a rebellious people (Ex 32:11-14; Nm 14:11-19; Dt 9:18-20), setting aside any personal gain, his own comfort, and the possibility of becoming the great leader of a great nation (Ex 32:10). He did not "switch teams." He did not sell out his own team. Rather, he fought for them until the end. Knowing that the Lord has set us aside for ministry, we should consciously guard ourselves from indifference, comfort, or personal interest in order to fight for the people whom God has entrusted to us and has called us to serve. Just like Abraham, we should courageously wrestle with God for their salvation. This is exhausting — just like Moses' arms were tired when he prayed during the battle (Ex 17:11-13).

Intercession is not for the lazy. We do not pray just to "meet our quota," to be at peace with our own conscience, or to experience an inner harmony that is purely aesthetic. When we pray, we are battling for our people. Is this how I pray, or do I get tired and bored, vowing not to get involved, and preferring that my own life be more peaceful? Am I courageous like Abraham in my intercession, or am I more like Jonah, bemoaning a leak in the roof instead of all those men and women who are victims of a pagan culture and "who do not know right from wrong" (see Jon 4:11)?

Jesus is very clear in the Gospel: "Ask, and it will be given you; seek, and you will find; knock, and it will be opened to you" (Lk 11:9). So that we understand clearly, Jesus gives us the example of the neighbor who keeps knocking in the middle of the night to ask for three pieces of bread, not worried by the fact that people might think he is a nuisance. He was just interested in getting the food for his guest. Let us also look at the woman in Cana (see Mt 15:21-28). She risks being thrown out by the disciples (verse 23) and being called a dog (verse 27) just to get what she wants: healing for her daughter. This woman knew how to bargain courageously in prayer!

The Lord promises the certainty of success to those who are persistent and insistent in prayer: "Ask, and it will be given you; seek, and you will find; knock, and it will be opened to you. For every one who asks receives, and he who seeks finds, and to him who knocks it will be opened" (Lk 11:9-10). He explains to us the reason for success: God is our Father. "What father among you, if his son asks for a fish, will instead of a fish give him a serpent; or if he asks for an egg, will give him a scorpion? If you then, who are evil, know how to give good gifts to your children, how much more will the heavenly Father give the Holy Spirit to those who ask him?" (Lk 11:11-13).

The Lord's promise to our faithfulness and constancy in prayer well surpasses what we can imagine. Beyond what we ask, he will give us the Holy Spirit. When Jesus exhorts us to be persistent in prayer, he sends us right into the heart of the Trinity, and, through his holy humanity, he leads us to the Father, and he promises us the Holy Spirit.

Let us return once again to the image of Abraham and the city he wanted to save. We are all very aware of the pagan dimension of the culture in which we live, a worldview that weakens our certainties and our faith. Daily, we witness how the powers of this world are constantly at work to displace the living God and replace him with the newest idols.

We see how the abundant life that the Father offers us in creation, and Jesus Christ offers us in the redemption (see Col 2:12-14), is being displaced by what accurately has been called "the culture of death." We also see how the image of the Church is deformed and manipulated due to misinformation, defamation, and calumny. We see how the media delights in talking about the sins and shortcomings of her children as proof that the Church has nothing good to offer.

In the media, holiness is not news; outrage and sin make the headlines. How can this be a fair fight? Who can fight against this? Do some of us possibly dream we can fight with merely human means, that with Saul's armor we could do something (see 1 Sm 17:38-39)?

Be careful, though. Our struggle is not against human powers, but against the powers of darkness (see Eph 6:12). Just as it happened to Jesus (Mt 4:1-11), Satan is seeking to seduce us, to disorient us, to offer us "viable alternatives." We

cannot afford ourselves the luxury of trusting. Granted, we
need to dialogue with all people, but we should not dialogue
with temptation. We need to find refuge in the power of the
Word of God like Jesus did in the desert. We need to resort
to begging in prayer: the prayer of the child, of the poor and
simple; the prayer of the son who knows he is a son and calls
upon his father for help; the prayer of the humble and poor
without any resources. The humble have nothing to lose. In
fact, God reveals the way to them (Mt 11:25-26).

It would be worthwhile to remind ourselves that this is
not a time for census, triumph, or harvest. The enemy has
planted weeds alongside the wheat within our culture, and
both are growing together. We cannot simply relax in our
complacency. We need to bend down and pick up the five
stones for David's sling (see 1 Sm 17:40). This is the time
for prayer.

Some of you may think that your bishop has turned
apocalyptic on you or has contracted a dose of Manichaeism.
As to being apocalyptic, I would say that I accept this since
the Book of Revelation is the book about the daily life of the
Church, and eschatology is being formed in each one of our
attitudes. As for Manichaeism, I do not see this because I
am convinced our role is not to separate the wheat from the
weeds. (The angels will do this on the day of the harvest.)
However, we do need to be able to discern this, and not be
confused, so that we can protect the wheat.

I wonder how Mary handled the daily contradictions
and how she prayed about them. What was in her heart when
she was coming back from Ain Karim and her pregnancy was
beginning to show? What was she going to say to Joseph?
What did she say to God on her trip from Nazareth to Beth-
lehem, or during the flight into Egypt? What did she say to
God when Simeon and Anna simultaneously broke out in

a hymn of praise, or when Jesus stayed back in the Temple? What did she say to God at the foot of the cross?

As she faced all these contradictions and many more, she prayed, and her heart grew tired in the presence of the Father [while] trying to read and understand the signs of the times in order to tend the wheat. When speaking about Mary's attitude, Pope John Paul II says that she experienced a "particular heaviness of heart" (encyclical *Redemptoris Mater*, 17). This heaviness of heart is nothing like the tiredness and boredom that I had mentioned earlier.

We can safely say that prayer, besides giving us peace and trust, also wearies the heart. It is the kind of weariness that comes from knowing that we are not deceiving ourselves; that we are taking a mature responsibility for our pastoral duties; that we are a minority in "this perverse and adulterous generation"; and that we accept daily the challenge to wrestle with God to save his people. The question then is this: Is my heart weary from courageous intercession, and, at the same time, do I know the peace of soul of one who relates to God as a friend? Weariness and peace go hand in hand in the hearts of those who pray.

Am I aware of the seriousness of my pastoral responsibilities, doing all that I can possibly do as a human being, and, at the same time, interceding in prayer? Have I tasted the simple pleasures of casting my cares unto the Lord in prayer (see Ps 55:22)? It would be so good if we could heed the advice of Saint Paul: "Have no anxiety about anything, but in everything by prayer and supplication with thanksgiving let your requests be made known to God. And the peace of God, which passes all understanding, will keep your hearts and your minds in Christ Jesus" (Phil 4:6-7).

These are more or less the thoughts I felt the urgency to share with you after meditating on the three readings for this Sunday, since together we are caring for God's faithful people. I ask the Lord to make us people of prayer just as he was when he walked among us. May he make us persistent beggars before the Father! I ask the Holy Spirit to immerse us in the Mystery of the Living God and to pray within our hearts. The second reading assures us that we already have the victory. Standing firm in this victory, let us press forward (see Heb 10:39) in our apostolic work, delving deeper and deeper in our relationship of friendship with God in whom we live in prayer. Let us grow in *parresia*, in courage, both in action and in prayer.

May we be mature men and women in Christ, but like children in the way we abandon ourselves to him. May we be men and women working to the very end and, at the same time, with hearts weary from prayer! This is what Jesus wants from us, and this is his call for us. Let us ask him to give us the grace to understand that our apostolic work, our difficulties, and our battles are not merely human, beginning and ending in us. It is not our battle, but God's battle (see 2 Chr 20:15). This is what moves us each day to spend more time in prayer.

Please do not forget to pray for me, since I do need it. May Jesus bless you, and may the Blessed Virgin Mary protect you!

# XX

# THE IMPORTANCE OF ACADEMIC FORMATION

ADDRESS OF CARDINAL JORGE MARIO
BERGOGLIO, S.J.,
ARCHBISHOP OF BUENOS AIRES,
DURING THE PLENARY SESSION OF THE PONTIFICAL
COMMISSION FOR LATIN AMERICA
FEBRUARY 18, 2009

~

## The Pastoral Goal of All Formation: In the Image of the Good Shepherd

The fourth section of *Optatam Totius*, the Second Vatican Council's Decree on Priestly Formation, gives us the end to which all priestly formation should be ordered in a way that is both systematic and harmonious:

"All the forms of training, spiritual, intellectual, disciplinary, are to be ordered with concerted effort toward this pastoral end (*hunc consociata ad finem pastoralem actione ordinentur*): the formation of true shepherds of souls after the model of our Lord Jesus Christ, teacher, priest and shepherd" (4).

Similarly, the *Document of Aparecida* says:

"There must be a seminary formation plan that offers seminarians a true comprehensive process — human, spiritual, intellectual, and pastoral — centered on Jesus Christ, the Good Shepherd" (319).

Thus the image of the Good Shepherd is the *analogatum princeps* of all formation. When speaking about the pastoral end as the ultimate end, both Vatican II and *Aparecida* understand "pastoral" in its preeminent sense — not the way in which it is different from other aspects of formation, but the way it encompasses all aspects of formation. All these aspects are part of the Good Shepherd's charity, since charity "is the form of all the virtues," as St. Thomas said, echoing St. Ambrose.[36]

In its most important sense, therefore, "formation" means "that Christ is formed within us," that we receive the form of Christ's love in us. This presupposes ongoing formation, in which we are always disciples and missionaries since, insofar as we are being configured to Christ the Good Shepherd as his disciples, we are empowered to go out as missionaries communicating this form of his love for us. This meaning of formation, in its most important sense, is the meaning that Paul expresses when he says: "My little children, with whom I am again in travail until Christ be formed in you" (Gal 4:19).[37]

### Formation for the Full Life of Jesus Christ

All formation, therefore, is ordered so that we may be good shepherds who are able to communicate the full life of Jesus Christ to our people, as *Aparecida* wishes:

> The People of God feel the need for disciple-priests: those who have a deep experience of God, are configured to the heart of the Good Shepherd, docile to the motions of the Spirit, who are nourished by the Word of God, the Eucharist, and prayer; for missionary-priests:

who are moved by pastoral charity which leads them to care for the flock entrusted to them and to seek out who have strayed furthest, preaching the Word of God, always in deep communion with their bishop, priests, deacons, men and women religious, and laypeople; for servant-of-life-priests: who are alert to the needs of the poorest, committed to the defense of the rights of the weakest, and promoters of the culture of solidarity. The need is also for priests full of mercy, available to administer the Sacrament of Reconciliation. (199)

*Aparecida* formulates these features of priestly identity as "challenges of the people of God to their priests." Our faithful want to have "shepherds for the people" and not a "state clergy,"[38] "teachers of life" that provide solid teaching on salvation and not "amateurs" who are preoccupied with defending their own reputation by discussing issues of secondary importance. To be good pastors and teachers who communicate life, we need from the beginning of formation a "solid spirituality of communion with Christ the Shepherd and docility to the action of the Spirit."[39]

*The Formation of Shepherds and Teachers.* To tend the flock in communion with Christ the Shepherd means not only caring for and leading the flock, but also feeding it and nurturing it, correcting it and healing it. For this reason, the title of shepherd also includes the title of teacher, a teacher who nourishes his flock by teaching the true way of life and by correcting its mistakes. The Good Teacher (see Mt 19:16) does not teach from the distance of the pulpit. Rather, he teaches as one who shepherds, by always being nearby, by always making himself available, by nurturing the flock in such a way that he always chooses what is truly nourishment and discards what is harmful, all the while sharing his life with his flock.

*Pastoral Ministry also Leaves Its Mark on the Academics.* In the language of Vatican II and Aparecida, "pastoral" is not in opposition to "doctrinal" but includes it. Nor is pastoral a mere "contingent, practical application of theology." On the contrary, Revelation itself — hence, all theology — is pastoral in the sense that it is the Word of salvation, the Word of God for the life of the world. As Crispino Valenziano says: "It does not mean adjusting our pastoral approach to conform to doctrine, but rather trying not to ruin what constitutes an original pastoral approach with doctrine. The 'anthropological stance' that we need to follow in theology without any misgivings or questioning is one that runs parallel to 'pastoral' doctrine: men and women receive revelation and salvation by perceiving the knowledge that God has of our nature and his condescension as Shepherd toward each sheep of his flock."[40]

This integrative concept of doctrine and pastoral approach (subsequently labeled "constitution" — a document that gives a permanent teaching — which was given not just to the dogmatic teaching of *Lumen Gentium*, but also to the pastoral teaching of *Gaudium et Spes*) is clearly reflected in the *Decree on Priestly Formation*. This decree emphasizes the importance of forming shepherds of souls, shepherds who, in union with the one Good and Beautiful Shepherd (beautiful in the sense that he leads by attracting and not imposing) who "tends his sheep" (see Jn 21:15-17).

## Solid Academic Formation

As regards the specifics of academic formation, I would like to stop and reflect for a moment about a characteristic that always comes up when talking about formation: soundness.

*Optatam Totius* emphasizes soundness of training in general and in each of its dimensions.[41] However, it particularly speaks about the need for educators to have and communicate solid doctrine:

"Since the training of students depends both on wise laws and, most of all, on qualified educators, the administrators and teachers of seminaries are to be selected from the best men, and are to be carefully prepared in sound doctrine, suitable pastoral experience, and special spiritual and pedagogical training" (5).

*Aparecida* quotes *Pastores Dabo Vobis*, [the apostolic exhortation in which] Pope John Paul II refers to "sound and serious formation" — a soundness that will lead priests to "grasp and incarnate the unique wealth of God's gift which is the priesthood and to express their capabilities and ministerial attitude, also through an ever more convinced and responsible insertion in the presbyterate."[42]

The soundness to which they refer is the soundness of the solid teaching of the Good Shepherd, who feeds his sheep with solid food, with words of eternal life.

### Soundness as a Property of Truth

What is not always sufficiently apparent is the fact that soundness is an important property of truth. According to the Hebrew way of thinking, truth is "*emeth*," which means to be solid, reliable, trustworthy, and worthy of faith. Christ's truth does not revolve primarily around intellectual "revelation," which is more like the Greek way of thinking. This revelation will be complete when "we shall see him as he is" (1 Jn 3:2), because now "we see in a mirror dimly" (1 Cor 13:12). Rather, Christ's truth revolves around adherence in faith, an adherence that involves our whole being — heart, mind, and soul. This adherence is an adherence to the person of Jesus Christ, "the Amen, the faithful and true witness" (Rv 3:14), in whom we can trust and whom we can support because he gives us his Spirit, who guides us "into all the truth"[43] and allows us to discern between good and evil. As the Letter to the Hebrews tells us:

> For though by this time you ought to be teachers, you need some one to teach you again the first principles of God's word. You need milk, not solid food; for every one who lives on milk is unskilled in the word of righteousness, for he is a child. But solid food is for the mature, for those who have their faculties trained by practice to distinguish good from evil. (5:12-14)

The soundness of which we are speaking, therefore, is participation in the priesthood of Jesus Christ, who "had to be made like his brethren in every respect, so that he might become a merciful and faithful high priest in the service of God, to make expiation for the sins of the people" (Heb 2:17).

Thus if someone thinks of abstract formulations or irrefutable syllogisms when he hears someone talking about solid doctrine, he is thinking within a rationalist paradigm that is different from the soundness of Christ's truth, which is that of the mercy and faithfulness of salvation.

## Soundness as Openness to the Mystery of Christ

If we read *Optatam Totius* carefully, we see that, when speaking about solid teaching, it says that we need to "align" the disciplines of philosophy and theology in order that our minds are "opened to the mystery of Christ":

> In revising ecclesiastical studies the aim should first of all be that the philosophical and theological disciplines be more suitably aligned and that they harmoniously work toward opening more and more the minds of the students to the mystery of Christ. For it is this mystery which affects the whole history of the human race,

continually influences the Church, and is especially at work in the priestly ministry. (14)

Soundness, then, is an openness — a solid openness, an openness that is faithful and unwavering, stable and permanent — to the mystery of Christ. It is an openness of the mind so that the fullness of life can flow in: "And this is eternal life, that they know you the only true God, and Jesus Christ whom you have sent" (Jn 17:3).[44]

In no way, therefore, is it a certain kind of doctrinal rigidity that seems to close ranks as a form of self-protection and that may end up excluding men from life. The Lord reproaches the Pharisees for this attitude when he says: "Woe to you, scribes and Pharisees, hypocrites.... You blind guides, straining out a gnat and swallowing a camel" (Mt 23:23-24). Quite the contrary, the soundness we seek for our priests is a human and Christian soundness that opens minds to God and to men.

One characteristic of solid truth is that it is always open to more truth, it is always open more widely and deeply to transcendent truth, and it then knows how to translate it pastorally in a way that will establish a dialogue with every man and culture.[45]

## Soundness That Dares to Proclaim the Word

The heart of this soundness revolves around the Word of God,[46] since sacred Scripture "ought to be, as it were, the soul of all theology"[47]:

"They are therefore to be prepared for the ministry of the word: that they might understand ever more perfectly the revealed word of God; that, meditating on it they might possess it more firmly, and that they might express it in words and in example" (*Optatam Totius*, 4).

We quickly see how training centered on the Word is not limited to intellectual understanding. Vatican II also stresses meditation — since it is a living Word that must be contemplated in a spirit of praise and worship — as well as expressing the Word, both through our words and through the witness of our life.

Soundness of the word comes from the constant interaction that takes place in the heart of the missionary disciple between internalization and implementation of what has been revealed to him. If the word is not put into practice, it is not solidified: it is as a house built on sand. The paradox is that this soundness is played out by taking risks, by using one's talents, by going outside of oneself to the outskirts of existence. It is not the soundness of a museum or of self-preservation. That is why it is essential for academic training to have a downward dimension — of planting and of being the leaven of reality — and, from there, to have an upward dimension — leading to the harvest of everything human that can be exalted and perfected by grace.

**Soundness of Humanistic and Philosophical Formation**
It is, perhaps, here that we find the crux of the problem with our current formation: contact with reality, both evangelization of the culture and inculturation of the Gospel, requires solid discernment.

Future shepherds need to enter into the heart of the culture of the people they will serve, and not merely on a superficial level, or with a fragmented knowledge of a reality that has been measured and modified by scientific research. Such scientific research is based on operational paradigms that do not seek to penetrate the heart of the matter but work according to its mode of operation. The image of reality that they offer is the projection of a desire for fragmented and multifaceted domination.

Instead, getting in touch with the living reality of the hearts of men and peoples requires a strong background in the human sciences, with particular emphasis on everything that allows a historical, symbolic, and ethical vision that encompasses the more analytical dimensions of scientific knowledge.

From a humanistic perspective, I would dare to say that the standard we seek is that those in formation will become over time shepherds who increasingly appreciate the wisdom of the people, and who, wherever they are, will connect symbolically and mystically with the unity of the nature and the transcendent mystery of God, expressed in a respect for the sacred and a devotion to the Holy One and to his saints. This path of inculturation of the Gospel and evangelization of the culture involves a journey along with the faithful, learning from them how to pray and how to love the true and living God. It is a path of discipleship in a communion that is always more and more inclusive — quite the contrary of those intellectual investigations in elite and self-referential circles that delight in discussing "disputed questions" instead of feeding the flock with solid nourishment.[48]

At the same time, in order for science to enrich formation and contribute its specific knowledge to this formation, which today has grown and become so specialized, solid philosophical formation is needed to open minds to the mystery of being and its transcendental properties.

## Philosophical Soundness as Openness to the Mystery of Being

Just as the soundness of the openness to Revelation has the Mystery of Christ as its object, which in turns opens us to the Mystery of the One and Triune God, so, too, does the soundness of a philosophical openness have as its object the mystery of being and each of its transcendental properties. Thus philosophical training must open students to the transcendental properties of being, where truth, goodness, and beauty, in its unity, are always open to God's truth, goodness, and beauty. It must seek the transcendent foundation of reality, where man's ultimate questions do not clash with each other in the different categorical systems, and are not always in conflict with each other, but allow fruitful dialogue with all thought that genuinely seeks the truth. *Optatam Totius* refers to this when it speaks of a "solid and coherent knowledge of man, of the world, and of God."[49]

As Hans Urs von Balthasar says:

> We can say, in general, that the usual relationship between philosophy and theology, long considered by the Catholic Church as a preparation for theology, has changed recently after a vast decline of scholastic philosophy. At present, theology seeks, rather, to be rooted in different ways in some of the so-called 'core' theologies. Or, if it does not, it does have as its presupposition the 'human sciences,' many of which, however, entirely lack the means to be an introduction to theology. (…) This results in a diffuse (theological) positivism, which extends — almost everywhere — to pastoral ministry. It then provides the faithful with considerations rooted in sociology that are actually a level below their 'unenlightened' piety, while 'enlightened' preachers think they have long surpassed those 'old ideologies' and, of course, cannot refrain from injecting their new knowledge into the catechesis of both young people and adults.[50]

In order to open ourselves up to the whole mystery of Christ, we need to overcome the widespread positivism that often abounds in theology. (Ideologies that are outdated in Latin America and the Caribbean are, at times, reissued elsewhere as though they are new.) In order to do so, we need to win back Christian philosophy from theology.

## Soundness as Discretion

The soundness of which we are speaking is not only the soundness found in an integral body of doctrine, which includes all of revelation in dialogue with the wisdom of all people from every culture. It is also the soundness of a well-tempered sword: the double-edged sword that discerns truth. Therefore, the soundness of the training of our shepherds should aim for spiritual "discretion," which knows how to test everything and keep what is good, as opposed to the temptation of "syncretism" of all kinds in today's world, beating around the bush disputing sterile questions or mixing the knowledge of disciplines that cannot be mixed.

As Erich Przywara says, "discretion" versus "syncretism."[51] There, where the "syn" of syncretism mixes incompatible and irreconcilable elements, and the "dis" of discretion imposes separation and clarity.

As Saint Anthony says, "discretion is the mother, guardian, and teacher of all virtues."[52]

Sound formation flows out of "discreet love," out of the discretion of the Good Shepherd, who knows how to carry his sheep to abundant pastures and founts of living water as he protects them from wolves, false shepherds, and other mercenaries.

# Notes

## Chapter I

[1] A meeting of the Latin American and Caribbean bishops in Aparecida, Brazil, May 13-31, 2007. This was one of five "general con-
ferences" that have been held over the years. The others were in
Puebla, Mexico; Medellin, Colombia; Santo Domingo, Dominican
Republic; and Rio de Janeiro, Brazil. At each one, a concluding
document was produced that Cardinal Bergoglio repeatedly refers
to in his talks.

## Chapter II

[2] The words are from a tango, written and composed by Enrique Santos Discepolo. Citing these words, Dr. Edward Mulholland made
the following observation in a Zenit report shortly after Cardinal
Jorge Mario Bergoglio's election as Pope: "His homilies are rich
in Scripture and in citations from the Fathers of the Church, but
he isn't above throwing out some local color, citing 1930's tango
composer and lyricist Enrique Santos Discepolo, and calling him
'*nuestro profeta porteño*' (our Buenos Aires prophet)."

## Chapter V

[3] "One day long ago / my hope died! / The downtown lights, / mag-
nets of folly, / took their cravings for a thousand misfortunes! / Perhaps one night their march will come to an end / the eleven o'clock
train, and my love will return!" (*El tren de las once*).

[4] Peter challenging the Lord after having confessed him as Messiah
(see Mt 16:16-23); James and John, the Sons of Thunder, wanting
Jesus to rain fire on the city that did not receive him (Lk 9:53-55).

[5] "Well, it all depends on the correct interpretation of the council or
— as we would say today — on its proper hermeneutics, the correct
key to its interpretation and application. The problems in its imple-

mentation arose from the fact that two contrary hermeneutics came face-to-face and quarreled with each other. One caused confusion, the other, silently but more and more visibly, bore and is bearing fruit. On the one hand, there is an interpretation that I would call 'a hermeneutic of discontinuity and rupture'; it has frequently availed itself of the sympathies of the mass media, and also one trend of modern theology. On the other, there is the 'hermeneutic of reform,' of renewal in the continuity of the one subject-Church which the Lord has given to us. She is a subject which increases in time and develops, yet always remaining the same, the one subject of the journeying People of God." As Cardinal Angelo Scola says, the pope does not oppose "discontinuity-continuity" or "rupture-continuity," but speaks of discontinuity and rupture versus a hermeneutic of reform or renewal in the continuity of the one subject-Church, specified as "the journeying People of God." (A. Scola, Credo Ecclesiam, in *Communio*, ed. Argentina, No. 1, Fall 2011, p. 5)

[6] "The first point is, to see the various persons: and first those on the surface of the earth, in such variety, in dress as in actions: some white and others black; some in peace and others in war; some weeping and others laughing; some well, others ill; some being born and others dying, etc. 2) To see and consider the Three Divine Persons, as on their royal throne or seat of Their Divine Majesty, how They look on all the surface and circuit of the earth, and all the people in such blindness, and how they are dying and going down to Hell. 3) To see Our Lady, and the Angel who is saluting her, and to reflect in order to get profit from such a sight." (*Spiritual Exercises,* 106).

## CHAPTER XV

[7] See *Hacia un bicentenario en justicia y solidaridad (2010-2016)*, 5. Document of the Bishops at the Closing of the 96th Plenary Assembly of the Argentinean Bishops' Conference, Pilar, November 14, 2008.

[8] Ibid.

[9] See *Para profundizar la pastoral social* 4. Letter of the Bishops in the Framework of the 88th Plenary Assembly, San Miguel, November 11, 2004.

[10] "Therefore, if it individualizes beyond a certain point, if it separates itself too radically from other beings, men or things, it finds itself unable to communicate with the very sources of its normal nourishment and no longer has anything to which it can apply itself. It creates nothingness within by creating it without, and has nothing left upon which to reflect but its own wretched misery. Its only remaining object of thought is its inner nothingness and the resulting melancholy." [4] "A life without meaning implies a life without social rootedness." Emil Durkheim, *Suicide* (Buenos Aires, Shapire Editor, 1971), p. 225.

[11] See *Para profundizar la pastoral social*, 4. Letter of the Bishops in the Framework of the 88th Plenary Assembly, San Miguel, November 11, 2004.

[12] *Documento de Santo Domingo*, 167. Fourth General Conference of the Latin American Bishops, October 12-28, 1992.

[13] See Pontifical Council for Justice and Peace, *Compendium of the Social Doctrine of the Church*, 2005, 153.

[14] Pope John XXIII, *Mater et Magistra*, encyclical on Recent Developments of the Social Question in the Light of Christian Doctrine, May 14, 1961, 219.

[15] Pope John Paul II, *Centesimus Annus*, encyclical on the Centennial of *Rerum Novarum*, May 1, 1991, 28.

[16] Pope Benedict XVI, *Caritas in Veritate*, encyclical on Integral Human Development in Charity and Truth, June 29, 2009, 75.

[17] Pope John Paul II, *Centesimus Annus*, encyclical on the Centennial of *Rerum Novarum*, May 1, 1991, 34.

[18] Ibid.

[19] *Document of Aparecida*, Fifth General Conference of the Bishops of Latin America and the Caribbean, Aparecida, May 13-31, 2007, 65.

[20] *Navega mar Adentro*, 85th Plenary Assembly of the Argentinean Bishops' Conference, San Miguel, May 31, 2003, 34.

[21] *Document of Aparecida*, 22.

[22] *Document of Puebla*, Third General Conference of Latin American Bishops, Puebla, 1979, 29.

[23] Pope John Paul II, Inaugural Address at the Seminario Palafoxiano de Puebla de los Ángeles, Mexico, January 28, 1979, III, 4.

[24] *Document of Puebla*, 29.

[25] Second Vatican Council, *Gaudium et Spes*, Pastoral Constitution on the Church in the Modern World, December 7, 1965, 29.

[26] Pope Benedict XVI, *Deus Caritas Est*, encyclical on Christian Love, December 25, 2005, 28.

[27] Pope Pius XI, *Quadragesimo Anno*, encyclical on the Restoration of the Social Order in Perfect Conformity with the Law of the Gospel in Commemoration of *Rerum Novarum*, March 15, 1931, 57.

[28] *Hacia un bicentenario en justicia y solidaridad (2010-2016)*, 5.

[29] *Afrontar con grandeza la situación actual*, 6b, the Bishops of Argentina, San Miguel, November 11, 2000.

[30] *Caritas in Veritate*, 36.

[31] Pope Paul VI, *Populorum Progressio*, encyclical on the Development of Peoples, March 26, 1967, 24.

[32] See *Caritas in Veritate, 40b*.

[33] *Hacia un bicentenario en justicia y solidaridad (2010-2016)*, 18b.

[34] Pope Benedict XVI, *Fighting Poverty to Build Peace,* Message for the Celebration of the World Day of Peace, January 1, 2009, 15.

35 Ibid.

CHAPTER XX

36 *"Ambrosius dicit, quod caritas est forma et mater virtu-tum"* (S.T., *De Virtutibus* 2, 3 sed contra); *"Caritas dicitur forma omnium virtutum, in quantum scilicet omnes actus omnium virtutum ordinantur in summum bonum amatum"* (corpus).

37 The word "formation," or "training," in the sense Saint Paul uses it, refers more to a gift from God as opposed to our own effort; Christ being formed in us centers on everything that is positive and gratuitous. The most common terms when speaking about education and formation are *"musar"* in Hebrew and *"paideia"* in Greek. *Musar* denotes the education of children that is both "instruction" (the gift of knowledge) and correction. God is the educator *par excellence* who forms his people through the law and through trials. The Greek concept of *paideia* has other overtones, awakening an individual's personality within a worldview that is well-defined. Today, it would correspond to a formation program that takes into account the challenges of today's world and corresponds to the paradigm of the modern world.

38 Cardinal J. M. Bergoglio, *El mensaje de Aparecida a los presbíteros*, Brochero, September 11, 2008, 18-19.

39 "Seminaries and houses of formation are no doubt a special setting, the school and home for the formation of disciples and missionaries. The initial formation time is a stage where future priests share life following the example of the apostolic community around the Risen Christ (…) preparing to live a solid spirituality in communion with Christ the Shepherd and in docility to the action of the Spirit, becoming a personal and attractive sign of Christ in the world, according to the path of holiness proper to the priestly ministry" (*Aparecida*, 316).

40 C. Valenziano, *Vegliando sul gregge*, Magnano, 1994, p. 16.

[41] "The discipline of seminary life is to be reckoned not only as a strong safeguard of community life and of charity, but also as a necessary part of the total whole training formation. For thereby self-mastery is acquired, solid personal maturity is promoted, and the other dispositions of mind are developed which very greatly aid the ordered and fruitful activity of the Church" (*Optatam Totius*, 11). "In order that the spiritual training rest upon a more solid basis and that the students embrace their vocation with a fully deliberate choice, it will be the prerogative of the bishops to establish a fitting period of time for a more intense introduction to the spiritual life" (*Optatam Totius*, 12).

[42] *Document of Aparecida*, 326; *Pastores Dabo Vobis*, 76.

[43] "When the Spirit of truth comes, he will guide you into all the truth" (Jn 16:13).

[44] As Pope John Paul II said in recalling his own formation: " '*Labia sacerdotum scientiam custodian …*' (see Malachi 2:7). I like to remember these words of the prophet Malachi, which are quoted in the Litany to Christ the Priest and Victim, because they serve as a sort of program for those called to be ministers of the Word. They must truly be men of knowledge in the highest and most religious sense of the word. They must possess and transmit 'knowledge of God' that is not only a repository of doctrinal truth, but also personal and living experience of the Mystery, in the sense that the Gospel of John states it in that great priestly prayer: 'And this is eternal life, that they know thee the only true God, and Jesus Christ whom thou hast sent' (John 17:3)." (John Paul II, *Gift and Mystery*, Colorado Springs, Colorado: Image Books, 1996, chapter IX.)

[45] Here we are following von Balthasar who speaks about the art of "openness" to all human truth and about the unity of the Truth of the mystery of Christ, showing that all words are, in essence, only one Word. He also speaks about the art of "clarifying transposition" that translates the one Word into many, thereby establishing horizontal relationships between thought systems and human truths.

This "reduction" of all truth to the mystery of Christ is not reductive and decadent syncretism, but rather a truly reconciliatory viewpoint that is part of Christ's work of reconciling all things in himself. (See H. U. von Balthasar, *Von den Aufgaben der katholischen Philosophie in der Zeit*, en: *Annalen der Philosophischen Ge-sellschaft der In nerschweiz*, 3 [1946-47], pp. 1-38.)

[46] "Sanctify them in the truth; your word is truth" (Jn 17:17).

[47] "(No one) believes that reading *[cátedra: explicación]* without anointing is sufficient, nor do they believe in speculation without devotion, investigation without admiration, observation without joy, activity without divine zeal, knowledge without charity, intelligence without humility, study without divine grace, reflective knowledge without divinely inspired wisdom." We have translated *"speculum"* as "reflective knowledge in keeping with the theory of *Itinerarium*" (*Optatam Totius*, 16. S. Cfr. Bonaventura, *Itinerarium mentis in Deum* prol., n. 4: 296).

[48] "If anyone teaches otherwise and does not agree with the sound words of our Lord Jesus Christ and the teaching which accords with godliness, he is puffed up with conceit, he knows nothing; he has a morbid craving for controversy and for disputes about words, which produce envy, dissension, slander, base suspicions, and wrangling among men who are depraved in mind and bereft of the truth, imagining that godliness is a means of gain" (1 Tm 6:3-5).

[49] "The philosophical disciplines are to be taught in such a way that the students are first of all led to acquire a solid and coherent knowledge of man, the world, and of God, relying on a philosophical patrimony which is perennially valid and taking into account the philosophical investigations of later ages. This is especially true of those investigations which exercise a greater influence in their own nations. Account should also be taken of the more recent progress of the sciences. The net result should be that the students, correctly understanding the characteristics of the contemporary mind, will

be duly prepared for dialogue with men of their time" (*Optatam Totius,*15).

⁵⁰ H. U. von Balthasar, *Regagner une philosophie a partir de la theologie,* in: *Pour une philosophie Chretienne,* Lethielleux, Paris, 1983, p. 175.

⁵¹ E. Przywara, *Criterios católicos,* San Sebastián, 1962, p. 103.

⁵² "*Unde Antonius dicit, quod discretio quae ad prudentiam pertinet, est genitrix et custos et mode ratrix virtutum*" (S.T., *In III Sententiarum,* Dist. 33, Quaest. 2, Art, 5 CO) in E. Przywara, *Criterios católicos,* p. 104. See Juan Casiano, *Colaciones* I, *Conf.* II, IV.